THE VILLAGE

By John R Cooper

A story based on actual happenings.

Dedicated to my wife Vicky in appreciation of her patience in putting up with me for over 60 years.

Forward

This is a story about a 'David and Goliath' battle between a group of elderly people living in a retirement village who were in the main aged pensioners and against one of Australia's largest companies. It will never be a best seller because it does not have any romance, sex, violence or foul language.

The story is based on transcripts of hearings and decisions of the Consumer Trader and Tenancy Tribunal, submissions, summary and decision of the District Court and minutes of meetings and other records of the Retirement Village Residents Association and a retirement village associated with the case.

The information contained within the story may be of assistance to residents of a retirement village who have to respond to a tribunal application brought by a village operator or who may themselves be anticipating taking their operator to the tribunal.

The names of some of the Characters have been changed to avoid embarrassment to any person or organisation, also the number of characters has been reduced to simplify the story.

CHAPTERS

Chapter 1

The Committee Meeting.

On the Mid-North Coast of New South Wales about half an hour from Port Macquarie a pelican rose off the waters of Pelican Lake which had been named after the many pelicans that made the lake their home. After gaining a reasonable height the pelican began to glide over the Pelican Waters Retirement Village towards Coffin Bay, so named because in the early days of white settlement in the area, the end of the bay which ran off the eastern side of the now Pelican Waters Retirement Village, was near the local cemetery and it was a common occurrence for the coffin bearing the body of a deceased person to be transported to the cemetery by boat rather than by horse and cart over unmade roads.

Pelican Waters is a retirement village of some 14 acres with 124 independent living units, together with a bowling green, swimming pool, library, gym, in-door bowls, club room, billiard room, meeting room etc.

A retirement village is a residential complex predominantly occupied by retired persons aged over 55 years who have entered into some form of contractual arrangement with the owner or operator of the village. At the time our story starts there are approximately 600 retirement villages across the State of New South Wales, accommodating more than 60,000 residents. Approximately half of the villages are operated by non-profit organisations such as churches and fraternal groups etc. The remainder are owned and operated by commercial, for profit, companies.

Residents "buying" into a retirement village do so under various types of contracts. Some enter into the purchase of a leasehold arrangement where the village operator owns the premises and the unit is leased from the operator under a long term lease which is usually 99 years or whole of life. Then there is the loan and licence arrangement where you pay an ingoing contribution up front in return for the right to occupy the premises. These types of villages are operated under the Retirement Villages Act (RVA) which is administered by the relevant State government. There are also a small number of strata villages that as well as being subject to the RVA are also under control of the Strata Act. There are also a small number of rental villages. The majority of these arrangements entail the payment of a deferred management fee which may be as high as 50% of the ingoing contribution when the unit is sold at the time of the termination of the lease and some also allow for the sharing of any capital gain.

The majority of people who decide to make the move into a retirement village, usually from a home on a quarter acre in which they have raised a family and lived for many years, do so in the belief that the remainder of their lives will be free from the mowing of lawns and painting etc. They also believe that the company who owns and operates the village will have the residents' interest and welfare as one of their principal concerns. In a minority of cases that is what happens.

As well as the ingoing and outgoing costs associated with living in a retirement village there is the monthly recurrent charge that covers the actual costs of running the village. Pelican Waters is a leasehold type village operated by a for profit company, the residents have paid a lump sum up front, called an ingoing contribution, to obtain their long term lease and as well as the monthly recurrent charge there is the deferred management fee which is worked out at 2.5% per year for a maximum of 20 years. The share of capital gain when the unit is sold is 50% each between the resident or their estate and the operator. The operating company gets its profit from the deferred management fee as well as their share of the capital gain.

It was the 29th March 2010, Jack Clarke was walking from the unit he shared with his wife of 50 years towards the village meeting room where the Residents Committee were to meet at 9.30am to discuss with Management the village budget for the coming year. The budget relates to the costs associated with the operation of the village which is financed from the monthly recurrent charge that all residents pay, anticipated expenses for the 2010-11 year were in the order of $410,000.

The pelican caught Jack's eye and he marvelled at the grace of its flight and he thought to himself, "If there is reincarnation after this life then I think I would like to come back as a pelican, and then I could keep an eye on my village". Jack regarded Pelican Waters as 'his village' he and his wife Janice had lived there in their retirement since moving from the Central West nearly 10 years ago and for the past seven years Jack had been President of the Pelican Waters Residents Association. Jack considered his position as President of the Residents Association to like being the Mayor of a small town, as well as being the main link between the residents and management he attended all of the social functions acting as MC and on Anzac Day he read the Ode prior to the BBQ, it was indeed Jack's Village.

Jack had a heart condition that had four years prior to moving to the village required open heart surgery involving a triple by-pass and what was then still an experimental procedure to try and address a severe problem associated with an irregular heartbeat. When he retired to Pelican Waters he did so with the aim of leaving behind his voluntary involvement in numerous committees, Boards and Councils which had occupied a lot of his spare time over many years. There had been over 10 years on the local Hospital Board progressing through the office of Treasurer, Vice Chairman and finally Chairman. As well there was a term on the Shire Council and as a Board member of the Regional Electricity Authority, then a number of years as a Director of the local Community Retirement Village. And it seemed he could not say 'no' when asked to be the Auditor for the district of the Presbyterian Churches and also the Family History Society, positions he held for many years.

So when Jack got to Pelican Waters he did so with the aim of 'not getting involved' in committees and such like. However, after a couple of years of observing the operations of this retirement village and its Residents Committee he decided to put his hand up for and was elected to the position of Residents Committee President at the 2002 AGM. Jack reckoned that any involvement in the Committee could not be anywhere near as stressful and demanding as his previous associations, there was no way that he could foresee what would await him. And so began an involvement that would require all the administration, communication and negotiating skills that he may have acquired over many years.

Pelican Waters Retirement Village was now owned and operated by Dollarvill Retirement Villages a recently floated public company which had grand designs of becoming a 'mover and shaker' in the retirement village industry and had purchased Pelican Waters three years earlier. When Jack and his wife had purchased their 'Whole of Life or 99 Years' Lease, the village had been in the hands of Park Family Partners Pty Ltd a privately owned family company which had developed the village. It appeared to Jack that Dollarvill Retirement Villages' main concern was their 'bottom line' and they had little regard for the welfare or concerns of the residents of their villages.

Jack had concerns that the village operating budget which was the primary matter to be discussed that morning included items that the residents were not being given a great deal of detail about and he anticipated a lively meeting with the representatives of Dollarvill.

Jack's primary reason for his participation in village affairs as President of the Residents Association was to ensure that all of the residents of his village received a fair go, particularly in relation to the monthly fee, known as the 'recurrent charge' that each resident paid to

9

cover the operating costs of the village. Retirement villages in New South Wales are under the overriding direction of the Retirement Village Act and Regulation, which legislation had recently been updated by the State Government. The main aim of the legislation was to provide for 'consumer protection' of residents living in the 600 or so villages throughout the State.

As Jack approached the meeting room he noticed that the Vice President was going through the door. Jan Gibson a lady in her 70's who as a single mum had raised three boys and during that time had worked two jobs to make ends meet. After the boys had left home Jan had put herself through university and had a Degree in Communication. She was a great asset to the committee and Jack appreciated her input. Jack also noticed an unfamiliar vehicle parked near the office so he presumed that representatives from Head Office had arrived.

Approaching from another direction were two of the committee, Michael Austin; a man in his mid-sixties who as an owner driver had operated heavy transport all of his working life. He was the sort of a no-nonsense bloke who called a spade a spade. He was accompanied by Joy English another of the committee who in her working life had had been a Stenographer and was a wiz at taking shorthand. Jack greeted these two with a friendly wave and a hearty 'good morning'.

On entering the meeting room Jack greeted Vice President Jan and also the Secretary, Robert MacTavish an 80 years old retired Police Superintendent of Scottish descent who was a stickler for detail and getting things right and Treasurer, Shirley Dunlop who had been a bookkeeper all of her working life and was analytic and precise in the way she looked after the residents Association's funds. Also seated was another of the committee, Trevor Dalton a grey haired man in his eighties who had worked in Work Place Relations and Conciliation dealing with Unions on work sites etc. for a large construction company.

Jack took his customary seat at the head of the table which had been set up to accommodate the anticipated eleven attendees of this meeting. After a few minutes the final member of the committee arrived and took his seat, Don Music was a tall balding man in his late seventies, a down to earth retired Police Sergeant with a world of experience in dealing with life's hard cases. Because of an old leg injury caused when a police horse backed into him during a ruckus with some university students back in the seventies Don now had difficulty in walking any distance and so he travelled around the village on a mobility scooter which he likened to riding a police motor cycle which he did for many years, and he had a reputation for driving the thing as if he were pursuing a speeding motorist.

Waiting till the appointed time to start the meeting Jack looked around at the members of his committee and reflected to himself how lucky he was to have such a diverse and talented group to assist him in what he anticipated might be a lively meeting.

Jack declared the meeting open and after a brief discussion as to what the committee would be looking for in the proposed budget Jack requested Michael Austin to go to the office and invite the Management Team to join the meeting.

After a short time Michael returned accompanied by the three Dollarvill representatives. Firstly there was the Village Manager, Rochelle Train, a lady with experience in the Retirement Village Industry having previously been the manager of a number of villages; she had been manager of Pelican Waters for about six months. Rochelle was accompanied by her immediate superior, District Manager Geoff Beard, a man in his early fifties dressed in an open necked shirt with short sleeves. Geoff was a likeable fellow with a no-nonsense personality who had come into village management from the Hotel Industry and usually supported the Manager by playing the 'hard man' who tackled a Resident on occasion when it had been reported that their dog had been observed to be in the village without a lead, which was strictly against the village rules. There were other misdemeanours such as driving in excess of the village's 10kph speed limit. Geoff thought that because he was only in the village once per week it was better for him to play the 'bad cop' and let the manager be 'Good Guy' and be liked by the majority of Residents.

There was also the Dollarvill NSW Operations Manager, Pierce Burken, in his early forties with a Degree in Business Management and about 10 years' experience in the Hotel Industry. He was dressed in a dark suit, although he had removed his tie in an effort to blend in with the attire of the committee; although the wearing of a suit was really not blending in. Dress in a retirement village was strictly informal and Residents only wore a coat and tie on special occasions, such as at the Anzac Day march, or as a mark of respect at a funeral. Jack's opinion was that Pierce Burken had not learnt that elderly retirement village residents needed to be spoken to and treated in a different manner to the manner in which he was obviously used to speaking to hotel patrons.

After the formalities of welcoming the management trio they took their places at the three remaining seats at the end of the table opposite Jack Clarke. Jack invited Geoff to go through and explain each line item in the budget, a copy of which had been handed to each of the committee members a couple of days earlier by the village manager.

Things did not start well when Treasurer Shirley sought clarification as to why the figures showed an anticipated deficit of over $17,000 for the year 2009-10; when she believed that there should have been a small surplus. On examination of the figures it appeared that there was a shortfall in the payment of the monthly recurrent charges, the committee were advised that the shortfall would have to be picked up by the residents in the coming year. Argument then followed along the lines that the non-payment of the recurrent charge was the responsibility of the operator because it resulted from vacant units. Pierce Burken was not having any of that so an impasse occurred.

The increase in the recurrent charge being requested was 4.4%; however the increase in the Consumer Price Index (CPI) for the past 12 months had only been 2.9% and as there were a number of expenditure line item calculations which were in excess of the CPI these were queried by the various committee members, after discussion the majority of these were accepted by the committee as being acceptable; however there were two line items that raised considerable discussion. The first was an amount exceeding $23,000 for insurance, the argument that the committee advanced was that as the residents did not own the buildings and they had no insurable interest in them, they could see no reason as to why they should be liable for the payment of such.

Secretary Robert then requested information as to just what the insurance policy covered, only to be advised by Pierce Burken that "the committee did not need to know that as it was a matter for the operating company". Pierce Burken also stated that because of Dollarvill's size and buying power the cost of insurance was a lot cheaper that it would be if the village was insured as a stand-alone operation. Trevor Dalton reminded Burken that when they purchased the village they called a meeting of residents to introduce themselves and stated that one of the advantages of being operated by a company such as theirs was that there would be certain advantages, financial and otherwise that would flow through to the residents.

The second item of contention was detailed as 'Corporate Recharge' for over $28,500. There was very little information regarding this line item, but in brief the committee were informed that it was to cover head office expenses associated with the operation of Pelican Waters.

After about an hour or so and a lot of argument about the budget the Dollarvill trio left the meeting.

It was the custom of the committee, in respect of the budget to make a recommendation to the residents as to whether they should approve or reject the statement of proposed expenditure and any increase in the monthly recurrent charge at a special budget meeting scheduled to be held at the end of May. The committee agreed that on this occasion they would not make any recommendation but leave it to the residents assembled on that occasion to listen to Dollarvill's proposals and make up their own minds.

There was a general consensus of the committee members that was summed up by Don Music when he said, "Jack, if that Pierce Burken thinks that this committee is going to recommend to the residents that the budget be approved then you can tell him that he's dreaming".

All agreed and Jack said that he thought that this could end up in a David and Goliath type battle.

Chapter 2

The Residents Budget Meeting.

During the month of April there were a number of emails from the committee to Dollarvill regarding various aspects of the budget, none of which resulted in the giving of any point by either the committee or response by the company. Then as required by legislation on the 1st May the village operator distributed to each resident a copy of the proposed budget detailing the expenditure and required income which resulted in a substantial increase in the residents' recurrent charge.

It was 9.30am on the 25th May 2010, the day of the residents' budget meeting. Jack Clarke took his seat on the small stage in what was known as the village meeting room. There were two tables placed end to end with six chairs placed facing the audience, on Jacks right was Secretary, Bob McTavish and alongside him on the end was Treasurer, Shirley Dunlop, the three vacant chairs on Jack's left were for the Dollarvill representatives. Jack observed that the meeting was well attended with 96 residents present and another 14 had sent proxy forms, which was well above average for a Pelican Waters residents' meeting, there were about 160 persons resident in the village. As Chairman, Jack declared the meeting open and went through the formalities of having the apologies read and accepted and the proxies for the meeting detailed by the Secretary.

Jack presented to the assembled residents a report detailing the committee budget meeting held with the Dollarvill representatives and the subsequent communications and highlighted the committee's concerns as to the several aspects of the budget that they were not happy. Residents were encouraged to question the management team on all aspects of the budget in order that all would have a clear understanding of what they were being asked to pay for in their monthly recurrent charges.

From the floor Trevor Dalton rose and moved "that management be allowed enter the meeting", this was immediately seconded by Don Music and on being put to the meeting the motion was carried. Jack requested Vice President, Jan Gibson to advise management that the meeting was ready for them. Jan soon returned followed by Rochelle Train, Geoff Beard and Pierce Burken. The three Dollarvill representatives took their places at the table with the Manager on Jack's left, alongside her was the District Manager and on the end sat the NSW Operational Manager.

After the formalities of giving welcome to the management team Jack requested that the proposed budget be presented. Geoff Beard the District Manager took the lead and went through the statement of proposed expenditure line by line. There were a number of questions from the floor regarding the cost of garbage disposal, the license fee for the jetty, the office telephone and other day to day expenses all of which were answered by management to the apparent satisfaction of the residents. However when it came to issues of insurance and management fees which had been given the fancy title of 'corporate recharge' together with the shortfall in the present year's recurrent charges there was much discussion and questioning by not only the Residents Committee Executive at the table but also from the floor.

Again Bob McTavish requested information as to just what the $23,000 for insurance covered, as previously stated by management at the committee meeting held some eight weeks earlier Pierce Burken advised that that was the company's private business and would not be divulged to the Residents. There was a distinct unfavourable murmur from the audience when they heard Pierce Burken's statement.

Shirley Dunlop sought details relating to the $28,000 allocated to 'corporate recharge'. Again it was Pierce Burken who answered, stating that the $28,000 was to cover the various head office expenses associated with the village operation, such as arrangement for the payment of accounts and wages, a proportion of the district manager's salary as well as general supervisory activities. A number of residents raised issues with Pierce Burken's explanations and it was very plain to Jack that the meeting was not going in the direction that the Dollarvill representatives had hoped.

After an hour Jack suggested that it appeared to him that the discussion with management had gone about as far as it could and thanked the Dollarvill representatives for their attendance and informed all present that under the Retirement Village Act which had recently been revised it was irregular for management to be present whilst any vote by residents was being taken and then told the Dollarvill trio that they would be advised as to the residents decision in due course. The trio departed and as they did so Jack observed a very cold atmosphere towards them in the room.

Following the departure of the Dollarvill representatives a number of residents raised their concerns about the sharp increase in the monthly fee and the attitude of Pierce Burken. Trevor Dalton then got to his feet and addressed the Chair, "Mr Chairman, I move that the statement of proposed expenditure be rejected". Jack asked was there a Seconder to the motion, to which question about 30 hands flew up. Upon putting the motion there was a sea of hands in the air indicating their support for the motion, on asking "any against" not one hand went up. "Motion Carried" declared Jack.

Trevor Dalton then again rose and said, "Mr Chairman, I move that the increase in recurrent charges be rejected". Again Jack went through the formalities of asking for a Seconder and taking a vote with the same result as previous. This was the first occasion to Jack's knowledge that the residents of Pelican Waters had rejected a budget, in the past they had always been able to come to a compromise with the operator and thus allow the manager to manage the village and the residents to get on with enjoying their retirement.

There was a considerable amount of talk between various residents at the meeting, Jack called the meeting back to order and advised the process that was to follow. Under the Retirement Village Act the committee was required to write to management advising that the budget had been rejected. Management would then have the opportunity to submit a revised budget for the Residents' approval, providing that it sought a lesser amount in recurrent charges than the original proposal, or the operator could take the matter to the Consumer Trader and Tenancy Tribunal commonly known as the CTTT or The Tribunal for determination by a Tribunal Member.

Among retirement village residents there had always been a reluctance to take matters to the tribunal, not because of the cost involved which if the residents did not have legal representation was minimal, but because operators would use the veiled threat that if the residents won then the operator would appeal the matter to the District or Supreme Court systems which could be very costly.

Jack advised the meeting that the committee would keep them informed as to any progress in the matter and closed the meeting. As the Residents dispersed and a few of the more able bodied began to stack the chairs away so that the room was cleared and the indoor bowls mat put down for that afternoons game Jack looked at the departing residents, many of whom he regarded as close friends. Two thirds of the residents were women and at least half of them were widows, ladies who did not want a fight with a multimillion dollar company, all they wanted was a quiet and peaceful remainder to their life.

There was little Betty Harper who had recently lost her husband of 56 years and who apart from a few years as a shop assistant after she left school had been a house wife all of her life, she had no experience with committees or dealing with large corporations. Holding Betty's arm as they left the room was Bernadette Tyson of similar age to

Betty who was also a widow and who for the 14 years she had lived in the village had been the chief seller of raffle tickets at the village's various social functions. Jack thought to himself that he did not want to put residents like these two old dears through any worry or turmoil such as a fight with the village operator, but then on the other hand he did not want to see Dollarvill take money off them that they should not have to pay.

There was a brief discussion amongst the committee members where it was decided that Jack and Bob would go to the office and advise management as to the outcome of the meeting which they did. Pierce Burken then seemed to realise that management had a problem and that the ball was now back in their court, he immediately requested Jack to convene a meeting of the committee to further discuss the matter with himself, Geoff and Rochelle.

The committee members were still standing outside the meeting room talking among themselves so Jack called them back into the meeting room which was now empty. A couple of tables were placed together with a suitable number of chairs around at which Jack took his customary place at the head supported on both sides by his Secretary and Treasurer with the remaining five members seated at the sides, three on one side and two on the other. The Dollarvill trio entered and took their seats at the table opposite Jack.

Pierce Burken commenced by stating that he understood the residents' position and that in a gesture of good will they were willing to reduce the total of the proposed expenditure of $410,000 by $994 which was the difference between this year's Corporate Recharge and last year's Management Fee. None of the committee showed any interest in such a proposal, Jack suggested that perhaps mediation of the matter might be the way to proceed; Pierce Burken stated that they would consider that proposal, the only alternative was to go to the Tribunal and the committee would be so advised in due course. So the hastily convened meeting ended and the trio left the room. Jack looked around the table at the committee and said, "Well boys and girls, I think we might have a fight on our hands, it might be best if we start to have a look at how this Tribunal business works."

Chapter 3

The Application.

The regular June monthly meeting of the Residents Committee was held as usual on the second Tuesday. Jack opened the meeting at 9.30am sharp as was his custom, all committee members were present, after dealing with the standard business of minutes, correspondence, accounts and reports Jack advised that there had been no communication received from Dollarvill regarding the rejected budget. There was considerable discussion as to the situation. Michael Austin, normally a man of few words put forward the suggestion that the best form of defence is attack; perhaps the committee should take Dollarvill to the Tribunal to get the matter resolved.

It was agreed that this was indeed a different approach and that maybe such a move could work in favour of the residents. Discussion about the proposal resulted in the committee agreeing to call a Special Meeting of residents to gain approval for such an action. That day notice of a Special residents meeting to be held in one week was issued.

One week later the day of the Special Meeting arrived, Jack reported to the meeting that there had not been any communication received from Dollarvill as to their intention regarding the rejected budget. The situation was discussed and it did not take long for the residents to agree that they should take the lead and make an Application to the

CTTT in an effort to have the matter resolved. A sub-committee comprising the President, Jack Clarke, Secretary, Robert McTavish and Treasurer, Shirley Dunlop were appointed to make the Application and develop the residents' case.

That afternoon Jack, Bob and Shirley met at Jack's unit and discussed the formulation of the Tribunal application. An application form was downloaded from the internet and filled out citing The Pelican Waters Residents Committee as the Applicant with Dollarvill Retirement Villages as the Respondent. The Application was made as follows:

The residents of Pelican Waters Village, represented by Jack Clarke seek orders as follows:

Under the Retirement Villages Act 1999:-

108 (1) An order in respect of a proposed variation of recurrent charges.

115 (1) An order in respect of the proposed annual budget for the next financial year.

> *1. That the nonpayment of Recurrent Charges for vacant units for the year 2009-2010 be made good by Dollarvill Retirement Villages.*

> *2. That the cost of Insurance be excluded from the 2010-2011 and future Budgets.*

3. That the cost of Corporate Recharge be excluded from the 2010-2011 and future Budgets.

4. That the Recurrent Charges be reduced by an amount equal to the addition of item 1 and the removal of items 2 and 3 from the proposed Budget and that regard is had to the payment of Recurrent Charges so far this year.

The following morning Jack took the Application to the Port Macquarie office of the Department of Fair Trading where it was duly lodged together with the payment of $5. As Jack was an Aged Pensioner the Application Fee was reduced from $80. Jack had never been involved in a Tribunal matter before so he sought information as to when cases were being heard in the near future that would be open to the public. The young lady behind the counter advised that there were a number of matters being dealt with the following Monday commencing at 10.00am and a matter relating to Newpark Residential Village was to be held at another venue in town in three weeks' time.

Two days later on the Friday morning the Tribunal Committee met at Jack's. When Bob arrived he said that he had just been to his letter box an there was an envelope from the Department of Fair Trading, upon opening the letter there was found advice that Dollarvill had lodged an Application with the Tribunal for orders relating to the matters almost identical to the four items of the residents' Application except that this Application sought to have the items included in the budget, whereas the residents' Application sought to have them excluded. It appeared that the Applications by the residents and the Operator had been lodged within the same week.

The date set for a Directional Hearing at the Port Macquarie office of the Department of Fair Trading was Monday the 16th August at 10.00am. There was no similar previous Tribunal case that could be found that might have given a guide as to how the Tribunal Member might rule in this matter. So Jack, Bob and Shirley set to work in formulating the evidence that would be required in presenting their case. A list of residents who would be requested to submit suitable affidavits was also drawn up.

The residents chosen to write affidavits all had expertise or experience that might add weight to the residents case, for example Jack's neighbour Frank Harrison, except for five years in the Navy during 1940 to 1945, had been in the Insurance Industry all of his working life, working his way up from a 16 year old office boy to State Manager of a large Commercial and Life Insurance company. Frank held the opinion that as residents have no insurable interest in the buildings then they should not be responsible for the cost of insuring them.

There were other residents who had a definite opinion that they should not be paying for any costs associated with Dollarvill's head office. Jack, Bob and Shirley reckoned that the more affidavits, evidence from previous budgets and the like would give weight to their case. And so the work of compiling a case that might sway the Tribunal Member in their favour commenced.

9.45am the following Monday Jack attended the tribunal room at the office of Fair Trading at Port Macquarie where a number of CTTT cases were to be held. Jack approached the counter and asked the young lady if it was ok for him to go into the tribunal room, her advice was to make himself known to the Security Officer at the door who would say if it was ok for him to enter. Jack explained to the Security Officer, a fairly large fellow a little overweight, dressed in a uniform of the type usually worn by court security personal the reason for his being there was to observe the proceedings in order that he might be familiar with the procedure in preparation for a Hearing that he was party to. The Security Officer indicated to Jack where he could take a seat.

Jack observed that the room was about seven by six meters in size. Along the back wall were a row of eight chairs, in front of these with a gap of about one and a half meters from the back chairs were two tables with a space between them with two chairs at each, all of the chairs were facing the other side of the room which had a table with one chair. There was also a single chair off to one side which Jack later learnt was for the Security Officer. There were two doors, the one that Jack had entered through and another diagonally opposite. Jack was the only one in the room.

At 10.00am the Security Officer stepped into the room and stood at the door, a minute later from the other door entered the Tribunal Member, a man in his mid-50's dressed in a grey suit and wearing glasses with a bundle of papers under his arm. On noticing Jack sitting in the room the Member beckoned the Security Officer over and nodding in Jack's direction asked quietly as to who this fellow was. The Security Officer explained Jack's presence to which the Member nodded 'ok'.

After the Security Officer had returned to the door the Tribunal Member said, "Case No RET 10/2675 Jackson Investments and Peter Wilson". The Security Officer announced to a small group waiting in the outer chamber. "All persons in the matter of Jackson Investments and Peter Wilson please come in."

The Tribunal Member introduced himself as Mr Robinson a Member of the CTTT adjudication panel assigned to hear today's cases. Robinson requested the Jackson representative to identify themselves and then likewise for Wilson to do the same. This turned out to be a matter where Peter Wilson had been renting a home unit from Jackson Investments, had not renewed the lease when it terminated and was therefore seeking the return of his Rental Bond of $800. Jackson claimed that the unit was not left in a clean condition and that he had to pay a cleaner to make the property suitable for the next tenant, also there was some minor damage to a wall that needed repair. Jackson presented photos and invoices and receipts for the work carried out to the total of $620. After hearing Wilsons side of the argument which was not very convincing, Robinson directed that Jackson Investments were to receive $620 of the bond and Wilson was to receive the remaining $180.

There were five other cases, four relating to rental bonds and another about a dividing fence. Jack observed that in each case the participant who presented the best evidence, particularly paper documentation, was inclined to have the better outcome. At 1.00pm the Member, Mr Robinson declared the proceedings of the day completed and Jack returned home a little more confident that he might be able to present a reasonable case on behalf of his fellow residents.

Three weeks later Jack attended another Tribunal Hearing which was held in a large room at The Boat Resort, a rather upmarket motel and conference facility on the banks of the Hastings River where the CTTT had hired the room for the day to accommodate the Hearing.

Residential villages are different to retirement villages in as much as the resident basically leases the land under which their dwelling, which is usually a transportable home, is situated. The resident is responsible for the upkeep and maintenance of their home and the property it sits on. The village operator looks after the common areas and facilities such as roads, swimming pool, activities rooms etc. for which the residents pay together with the rental fee for their site a recurrent charge, usually based on a weekly amount.

Jack arrived shortly before 10.00am, the appointed hour for the Hearing to commence. There were a number of mature age people in the lobby area. Jack spoke to a couple in their early sixties and asked if they were connected with the Newpark Village matter, they advised that they were and that the matter related to an increase in their weekly charge which was above the CPI.

At 10.00am the Security Officer called for all involved in the matter of Newpark Village to go to room 102 on the first floor. Jack joined about sixty or so people who went into room 102 and took a seat in the back seventh row of ten chairs in each row. In front of the rows of chairs there were two tables with three chairs at each facing a third table with one chair at the front. Seated at the front table was Mr Robinson who Jack had seen three weeks before at the CTTT Hearings held at the Office of Fair Trading. Two women and a man took the three chairs at the table on the right and a man and a woman took their place at the other table.

Mr Robinson commenced the proceedings by stating that the Hearing had been called to resolve the matter between Newpark Village Pty Ltd and fifty five residents who had each made an application seeking orders that the increase in the weekly charge be restricted to an amount equal to the CPI. Evidently under the Residential Parks Act each resident has to make a separate application in such matters, whereas under the Retirement Village Act the Residents Committee or its Chairman can make an application on behalf all of that village's residents.

The Tribunal Member stated that as each Application was identical he would deal with the hearing as one matter and make any orders as applying to all. He then asked who was representing the Applicants, to which one of the ladies at the table on the right introduced herself as Muriel Wake of the Affiliated Residential Park Residents Association Inc. and sought leave to represent the applicants. Such was granted and the Member then asked who was representing the Respondent to which the fellow at the other table rose and introduced himself as William Browning, a Director of Newpark Village Pty Ltd and manager of the village.

The residents' representative presented arguments against any increase above the CPI and William Browning argued that the increase as requested was necessary to meet the increased expenditure relating to the operation of the village. After about a half hour of statements for and against Mr Robinson stated that if he was to rule on the matter that there would be one of the parties who would not be happy and suggested that Ms Wake take instructions from the Applicants and that she and Mr Browning remain in the room whilst everyone else retired and try to resolve the matter to the mutual benefit of all and that the Hearing would be resumed in 45 minutes.

All except Ms Wake and Mr Browning retired and moved to the lobby area. After thirty minutes Jack went back upstairs to the first floor where he found Mr Robinson in the passage way. Jack approached the Member and introduced himself and explained that he had nothing to do with the present matter before him and that he was there to gain experience for a future hearing and asked for the Member's opinion on several points of procedure, to which Mr Robinson was most helpful.

Shortly after the Hearing was resumed and the parties informed the Member that they had agreed that instead of the $7.35 per week that had been proposed by the village operator, they had agreed that the increase would be $4.20 which was slightly above the CPI. The Member then issued orders in line with the agreement reached and closed the Hearing.

Jack left the Boat Resort feeling that the morning had not been a waste of time and that he was better equipped for the battle that was to come.

During July and early August Jack, Bob and Shirley put together the paperwork in respect to the residents' case which they presumed had to be presented at the Directional hearing which was scheduled for Monday, 16th August. On the preceding Friday Bob came to Jack and handed him a letter from Dollarvill which stated that they had considered the situation in respect to the unpaid recurrent charges that formed part of the forthcoming Tribunal case and had decided to accept the residents' claim that the Operator was responsible to make up any shortfall.

After reading the letter Jack turned to Bob and said, "Well Mate, it looks as if the residents have just picked up $17,000." That day Jack informed each of the committee members of this new development.

Chapter 4

The Tribunal Direction Hearing.

Monday, 16th August arrived and at 9.50am Jack, Bob and Shirley together with the five remaining members of the residents committee entered the office of the Department of Fair Trading in Port Macquarie. Shortly after the Dollarvill representatives, Pierce Burken, NSW Operations Manager, Geoff Beard, District Manager and the Village Manager Rochelle Train entered. All were very cordial with greetings and handshakes between the major players. Pierce Burken asked Jack if he had received their letter regarding the unpaid recurrent charges that they were now willing to accept as their responsibility, to which Jack replied that he had and that the committee were hopeful that the remaining matters could be solved as simply.

The same Security Officer who Jack had previously had contact with when he attended a Tribunal Hearing a couple of months ago was there and when he saw the eleven people assembled in the Fair trading office he ushered them all into the tribunal room. Jack and Bob took a seat at the first table with Shirley and the remainder of the residents' committee seated behind them. Pierce Burken and Geoff Beard took the two seats at the other table with the village manager seated behind them.

At 10.00am the door on the side of the room opened and through it came the Tribunal Member, a man in his early 60's, about 180cm tall,

33

of slight build with greying hair and glasses. He was dressed in a dark suit with pin stripes and looked like a typical solicitor. Jack later found out that the Member was a registered solicitor who had been employed by the CTTT for many years and was one of only a handful of Tribunal Members who had the title of 'Senior Member'.

The CTTT Member commenced proceedings by introducing himself as Jeff Jones, Senior Tribunal Member. He stated that this morning's proceedings were a Directional Hearing and therefore no evidence would be taken on this day. Mr Jones also advised that he would allow only one spokesperson from each side to speak. He stated that as the two Applications from the two parties had brought a complaint against each other for basically the same matters it was his intention to deal with both matters at the same time and treat the proceedings as one and that he would treat the residents committee as the Applicant and Dollarvill Retirement Villages as the Respondent.

The Senior Member then turned his attention to Jack and Bob and asked who was representing the Applicant? Jack raised his hand and said, "I do Mr Jones, my name is Jack Clarke and I am the President of the Pelican Waters Residents Association."

Mr Jones said that he noted that Jack Clarke had signed the Application on behalf of the residents committee; however, he would need documentary evidence that Jack Clarke had been appointed by the residents to speak on their behalf and suggested that at the full hearing to be held at a date to be decided that a copy of the minutes of a meeting where the residents had given Mr Clarke such authority be included in the documentation. Jack assured Mr Jones that that would be no problem. With that Jack was allowed to continue as the residents' representative.

The member's attention was then directed to Geoff Beard and Pierce Burken, seated at the other table and requested for the Dollarvill Retirement Villages representative to state his name and authority. Pierce Burken gave his name and said that he was the NSW Operational Manager, employed by Dollarvill Retirement Villages to which Mr Jones thanked him.

Mr Jones then stated that the Application listed three issues. The nonpayment of Recurrent Charges for vacant units for the year 2009-10, Insurance and Corporate Recharge.

Jack advised that the matter of accountability of unpaid recurrent charges had been resolved. This was achieved by Dollarvill amending the Amended Draft Financial Statement which was received last Friday and which now recognises that the financial position for the year 2009-2010 now correctly shows an anticipated surplus of $482, whereas previously the Budget papers had in the opinion of the Residents' Committee had incorrectly shown a deficit of $17,829. Therefore for practical purposes Dollarvill would not charge the residents for the vacant units.

The Senior Member then asked Pierce Burken if this was correct to which he replied in the affirmative. Mr Jones then noted that the item of recurrent charges had been resolved and was therefore removed from both Applications. He then went on to say that in matters such as these unless the parties could come to some mutual agreement then there would be one winner and one looser and he suggested that if Mr Clarke was confident that he had the authority to negotiate on behalf of the residents then it would be appropriate for Mr Clarke and Mr Burken to go to the privacy of the adjoining room and try to negotiate a settlement of the matter. Jack advised that as the full Residents Committee were present he would take their directions into the negotiations.

With that the Senior Member adjourned the Directional Hearing. Jack conferred with the committee who unanimously advised that they were not inclined to give way in any substantial manner; however, they authorised Jack to enter into negotiations to try and resolve the situation.

Jack and Pierce Burken went into the small room set aside for such occasions; it was sparsely furnished with a table and four chairs. The two men sat opposite each other, the atmosphere was cordial although a little tense. Pierce Burken opened the conversation by saying that he could offer no reduction in the cost of insurance; however, he again offered a reduction of $994 in the Corporate Recharge amount to make it the same as last year. Jack said that he could not accept that as that offer had previously been rejected by the committee and also by the residents at the special meeting held at which the decision to take the matter to the Tribunal had been considered.

It was clear that this mediation attempt was not going to resolve the matter. Jack and Pierce left the small mediation room and returned to the Tribunal room where Jack informed Mr Jones that he and Mr Burken had not been able to reach any agreement. Jack advised the Member that the residents' representatives were willing to agree that any order handed down by the CTTT will be accepted and not appealed and suggested that Dollarvill might agree to the same. Mr Jones stated that it was only possible to accept such a proposition if both parties agreed. Pierce Burken advised that Dollarvill would not accept the suggestion and their options would be left open in this regard.

Jack then suggested that the Tribunal might consider the matter based on the written evidence with a written decision, thus avoiding the need for Mr Jones and Dollarvill Representatives to travel up from Sydney. The Member advised that both parties would have to request this in writing; Pierce Burken stated that he would not agree to this proposal. The Member advise that he would set aside a full day for a Hearing, which would be advised; however it would be sometime after the 21st September. Mr Jones then adjourned the Application and set the 7th September as the deadline for Pelican Waters Village Residents to submit their Application, two copies, one for the Tribunal and one for Dollarvill. The Application had to contain all evidence and arguments and that any additional items would probably not be admissible at a later date. Dollarvill will then have till the 21st September to reply to the residents' evidence.

Before Jack left the Fair Trading office he spoke to the young lady behind the counter and suggested that when organising a venue for the Hearing that a room much larger than the hearing room there would be required as there would be a fair number of residents who would want to be present to witness the proceedings.

All parties then left the Fair Trading office and went their separate ways. Jack had advised his committee that he would prepare a written report for distribution to all of the village residents. Jack also stated to the committee that he thought the Tribunal Member appeared to be on the ball as far as his knowledge of the Retirement Village Act and Regulation was concerned and that he believed that they would get a fair go at the Hearing.

Chapter 5

Preparation for the CTTT Hearing

Thursday morning, three days following the Directional Hearing Jack, Bob and Shirley met at Jack's unit to review the documentation that they had compiled prior to last Monday. Jack's wife Janice was not interested in all of this business of committee meetings and Tribunals etc., because she, like her husband had moved into the village with the aim of a quiet life without any hassles, and she had been mostly successful in following that aim.

Janice busied herself with a small garden at the front of their unit and another area at the rear between the unit and the Lake which was only about 80 meters from them and of which they had a great view. Janice had two other main interests in her life, one was her family, she and Jack had had five children, four boys and a girl and now had 14 grandchildren. Her other love was Samson, a rather handsome Chihuahua which had been acquired some four years earlier after the death of one of their sons which had left a great hole in their lives. So Janice excused herself left the unit and went off with Samson.

The Tribunal Trio set to work reviewing each document that had previously been developed in support of their case, making amendments where necessary, listing new items and possible statements that might be of assistance. They also researched previous Tribunal cases, although Tribunal decisions did not set a precedent at law the Tribunal Members were expected to be consistent in their rulings. However no previous cases that might be of assistance could be found.

Also considered was assistance or advice that they might obtain from external sources without incurring any costs. Jack suggested that the first point of call should be to the Retirement Village Residents Association, (RVRA) which was the only organisation wholly representing retirement village residents in NSW. The RVRA is a not-for-profit association, non-government and non-commercial with no affiliations outside the interests of village residents. The association is run by volunteers elected annually. Funding for the RVRA is wholly from membership subscriptions.

Jack had had previous contact with the RVRA committee a couple of years earlier when he and Bob McTavish had put together a submission to the State Government at the time the Retirement Village Act was being reviewed. They had sent a copy of their submission to the RVRA and as a result Jack had been invited to join a select group from the RVRA committee who were meeting with the then Minister for Fair Trading and also the Shadow Minister.

It was agreed that Jack would send an email to the President of the RVRA detailing the residents' rejection of the budget and the case being presented to the Tribunal for their comments. He was also to follow up with a phone call, which was done the following day.

Malcolm McKenzie a retired accountant and a resident of a village at Camden was the President of the RVRA. Jack spoke to him on the phone for some time with Malcolm agreeing wholeheartedly with the action that the Pelican Waters residents were taking and offered moral support although there was not much more that the RVRA could do at that time. However Malcolm did advise that their honorary Solicitor Peter Hill might be of assistance but this would most probably come at a cost. Peter Hill was a man in his mid-thirties who ran a small legal Practice on the Central Coast where there were a number of Retirement Villages and this is where his expertise in the Retirement Village Act and Regulation was developed. In fact he was one of the very few Solicitors in NSW with any knowledge of the Retirement Village Industry who was prepared to represent Retirement Village Residents.

Jack, Bob and Shirley decided that at this time they would rely on what they perceived as the strength of their case which was that the residents had not been given sufficient detail in respect to insurance and management fees which had been given the fancy name of corporate recharge. They noted that the Application that Dollarvill had originally lodged was in the name of Dollarvill Limited, whilst all of the documentation, including and particularly the lease documents, were in the name of Pelican Waters Retirement Village Pty Ltd. They decided to keep this inconsistency in mind as it might present an opportunity to score a point during the Hearing.

When completed the Application to the CTTT was contained in a folder with some 300 pages consisting of copies of meeting minutes, a lease document together with a disclosure statement, the budget and it's attachments, 11 affidavits detailing various opinions and statements, letters to and from Dollarvill, together with all the documents relating to the Application and Directional Hearing. Five copies of this large volume had been put together; one for Jack, Bob and Shirley, one for the Tribunal and one for Dollarvill. The latter two were duly posted off in time to meet the deadline of 7th September as given at the Directional Hearing. The trio agreed that there was not much more they could do until the response to their submission had been received from Dollarvill which was due on the 21st September.

On the 20th September Jack received a letter from the CTTT advising that Dollarvill had requested an additional 14 days in which to submit their response. Jack was able to meet with Bob and Shirley that afternoon and after discussion it was decided that the best thing to do would be to agree to Dollarvill's request because by the time a response got back to the CTTT objecting to the request it would be past the allocated date anyhow, also by not being hard to get on with might put the residents in good standing.

A letter was received from the CTTT on the 23rd September advising that an extension had been granted to extend the Dollarvill response time till the 1st October. Notice was received on the 28th September advising that the Tribunal Hearing was set down for the 8th November at 10.00am in the Hastings Room at The Boat Resort, Port Macquarie. Jack was pleased that a large venue had been allocated and made a mental note to send out a note to the residents requesting that as many as possible attend on the 8th and would arrange for a driver for the village bus to accommodate those who did not have access to a car.

As there had been no response received from Dollarvill by the 6th October, five days after the deadline, Jack phoned the CTTT to ascertain if they had received Dollarvill's response; their advice was that they had not. Jack reported the situation to the Bob and Shirley and it was agreed that if nothing was forthcoming in five days then Jack was again to phone the CTTT which he did and was advised that they had received Dollarvill's response on the 7th, four days earlier.

Jack's immediate thought was that Dollarvill was playing 'silly buggers' and that enough was enough. He immediately went to the village office and requested the manager Rochelle Train to make enquiries at head office as to the whereabouts of their response and convey to them that the residents were not very happy about being mucked around. After a short time Rochelle phoned Jack extending the company's apologies and advised that Dollarvill's response would be delivered by special courier the next day. Jack ended the phone call by stating that he was looking forward in great anticipation to receiving a document that had taken so long to prepare.

The following day, 12th October, about midday the village manager knocked on Jack's door and handed him a folder on the cover of which noted the case number and the heading "Respondent's Documents'. The folder which apparently had been compiled by someone with a legal expertise contained some 200 pages, about a half of these were a copy of Dollarvill's standard lease and memorandum

43

documents. There was also a copy of the proposed budget papers and various letters to and from the Residents Committee. The index to the document listed three witness statements, one from Pierce Burken, one from Amam Lam whose title was Financial Controller and one from Rochelle Train, on examination Jack discovered that the statement from the village manager was missing.

Jack made two copies of relevant pages leaving out the 100 or so lease and budget pages as these were already in the residents' application and delivered then to Bob and Shirley and arranged that they would meet in three days' time to consider the response. A phone call was made to the village office with advice that the Manager's statement was not included with the response document. The following day Rochelle delivered three copies of her witness statement to Jack.

Friday, 15th October, Jack, Bob and Shirley met and went through Dollarvill's response document. The response commenced with a 'Submission of the Respondent' document consisting of sixteen pages of details relating to the companies' structure, a history of events leading up to the Directional Hearing, operating multiple villages, village contracts and a lot of what Bob referred to as 'filler statements' used to put bulk into the document. One such item was a repeat of a lot of text straight from the budget papers that were also included in full elsewhere in the response.

The witness statement of Pierce Burken stated that he was 'General Manager of Operations' for Dollarvill Ltd, a publicly listed company operating 30 retirement villages with over 580 employees. He stated that his role as Operations manager was to oversee the proper operations, compliance and administration of the retirement villages and that as part of his duties he was responsible for sourcing the insurance for the villages and to determine the corporate recharge paid by each village. The statement then went on to detail the various sections that made up the corporate recharge; Human Resources, Payroll, Finance, Information Technology and Administration.

Jack, Bob and Shirley noted that the detail given for the five items encompassed by corporate recharge was much more detailed than that in the budget papers. They were surprised that attached to Burken's statement was a quote for insurance of the village as a 'Stand Alone' policy, the premium was quoted at $48,851 whereas the insurance amount in the budget was $23,100. This was provided in an effort to show what a great deal the residents were getting with the aid of Dollarvill's buying power.

However on examination of the detail in the policy it was found that not only was the policy covering the items as per the Retirement Village Act of damage, costs incidental to the reinstatement or replacement of insured buildings, public liability, and provides for the reinstatement of property to its condition when new, but was also covering such things as; gross profit, works of art and curios, money to the value of $20,000 consequential loss and head office corporate salaries insured for 100% for three years. The trio were astounded that these extraordinary items were included in the policy and decided to make this issue one of the main points of contention in arguing of their case.

They then turned their attention to the witness statement of Amam Lam, Dollarvill's financial controller. It consisted of seven pages and contained a lot of the same information that was contained in Burken's statement. Lam went into detail about how the corporate recharge was allocated among the thirty villages on an hourly basis and as it was perceived to have been used. Lam also mentioned that corporate recharge contained an amount of $3,500 for an audit fee. The mention of an audit fee raised the eyebrows of Shirley; she reminded Jack and Bob that when Dollarvill acquired Pelican Waters Retirement Village their management team at a meeting of residents had stated that one of the benefits of their management would be that the residents would no longer have to pay for an auditor each year. A note was made to add this issue to their argument.

The final witness statement contained in the response was that of the village manager, Rochelle Train. The document was of eleven pages and dealt totally with Rochelle's duties as village manager which had absolutely nothing to do with the matter before the Tribunal and offered nothing to support Dollarvill's case.

Jack voiced the opinion that he thought that the case they had presented had a lot of weight to it whilst Dollarvill's response had given them further ammunition particularly in respect to the extra items covered in the insurance policy and the inclusion of audit fees hidden in corporate recharge. It was agreed that the next job was to prepare a statement for verbal presentation at the Tribunal Hearing which they would do the following week.

Bob McTavish when leaving Jack's unit turned and said, "Well Jack, we might not have known much about Tribunals and how they work before all this started, but I reckon that by the time we are finished we'll be bloody experts."

Jack called a meeting of the full Committee to bring them up to date as to where he Bob and Shirley had got to in their preparation for the Tribunal Hearing. He also raised the question of what he should do if there were a negotiation and Dollarvill were to ask for a compromise of some sort. After looking at a breakdown of the costs of insurance and corporate recharge and what the Committee considered might be a fair thing, it was agreed that if Dollarvill would consider accepting a reduction of $15,000 in the combined cost of those two line items which were shown in the budget as $51,694 down to $36,694 then Jack would be authorised to accept such an offer.

For a number of years it was Jack's custom each Monday afternoon at about 4.00pm to visit his neighbour Frank where a scotch or two would be partaken of and the troubles of the world and in particular the Australian cricket team would be discussed. When Dollarvill Retirement Villages Ltd had become owners of Pelican Waters Village they had advised residents that as they were a public company shares in the company were available to be purchased. Frank had taken up the offer and purchased $10,000 worth. Frank told Jack that he had read in the Financial Times that Landbuild Limited a large

Australian property company were looking to take over Dollarvill with a share offer. Jack and Frank discussed as to whether Landbuild would be aware of the impending CTTT case, after discussion they concluded that the matter would be so small in the scheme of things as far as Landbuild were concerned that it would not matter.

Chapter 6

The CTTT Hearing – Part 1.

Monday, 8th November 2010 arrived, Jack and Bob drove to the Boat Resort in Port Macquarie and arrived there about thirty minutes before the Hearing was due to start at 10.00am. Already there were several of the village residents in attendance an as minutes ticked by the more and more arrived including the village bus which Michael Austin had driven in with seventeen residents on board. There was no Security officer present, evidently the CTTT did not anticipate a riot or such like and presumed that all parties would behave themselves.

Jack knew that the Hearing was to be held in the Hastings room which is where the matter involving the Newpark village had been held which he attended as a spectator about six weeks earlier. Jack and Bob made their way up the stairs to the allocated room which they found set up with about 70 chairs for the audience with two tables in front each with three chairs and another table right at the front with one chair facing the rest. Jack went to the top of the stairs and beckoned for his fellow residents to come up and to take their seats in the room.

Shortly before 10.00am from a side door entered four Dollarvill representatives, the village manager Rochelle Train, the district manager Geoff Beard, the NSW operational manager Pierce Burken and Ron Chaplin, who Jack knew to be the Dollarvill business manager from Sydney. Jack had previously surmised that it had been Chaplin who had put together the Dollarvill response as all of the documents had a certain legalise about them. The three men took the three chairs allocated at the table on the left of the room, Rochelle picked up a spare chair from the side of the room and placed it at the end of the table and sat next to Geoff Beard. Chaplin was seated at the other end of the table with Burken between Chaplin and Beard.

Jack looked around the room and did a quick count and found that besides himself Bob and Shirley who had taken up seats at the table on the right with Jack in the centre, that there were fifty four Pelican Waters residents present. Jack reckoned that that was a goodly number and was sure that their presence would make an impression on the Tribunal Member.

Jack left his seat and went to the Dollarvill table and shook hands with the four Dollarvill representatives and expressed the sentiment that whatever the outcome of today's proceedings he hoped that in the future a good working relationship could be established between the residents and management. There were nods of agreement from Chaplin and Burken; Geoff Beard said that he was sure that in future all would work towards that end. Jack returned to his seat.

A couple of minutes later Senior tribunal Member, Jeff Jones entered the room and took his place at the front table. He commenced by saying that he did not have his files for today's hearing, he expected them to be delivered at any minute but in the meantime did anyone have a spare copy of the Application and the Response. Geoff Beard handed Jones his copy of Dollarvill's response and Shirley handed him her copy of the application, he then took a small recording device from his pocket, held it up in order that Jack Clarke and Pierce Burken could see it, then placed it on the table. No one in the room could have known just how important the recording made that day would be in the future.

The proceedings commenced with Jones saying. "Good morning, ladies and gentlemen, my name Jeff Jones, member of the Consumer Trader & Tenancy Tribunal. Firstly, I would like to apologise for keeping you all waiting. I can make a lot of excuses. King George VI once famously said "*I'm sorry I'm late but I didn't start on time.*" That's not my excuse I did start very early this morning but through one thing and another I have turned up late and without the files. The parties have kindly provided copies of some of the documents, that may cause some difficulties throughout the day but anyway I think it's important for us to get started."

"Now, Mr Burken, you're appearing for the operator?" Pierce Burken replied that that was correct.

Jones then turns his attention to Jack, "And it's Mr Clarke isn't it?".

Jack replied "Yes" to which Jones continued, "You're appearing for the --".

"Residents" Jack replied.

Looking at the two folders in front of him Jones continues. "Residents. O.K.. Now, there is no microphone provided here and I will try and elevate my voice and I hope you can hear what is being said but the reality is that this isn't intended to be a spectator sport. I know you're here because you're interested but the facilities are not ideal and that's no reflection of the management of this place. You know, we usually operate in a court room set up and that often means - also means that parties in a court room are unable to hear the finer points of what's going on between the adjudicator and the parties themselves. So, if that happens I apologise but you've got a pretty good idea of what we're here for and the respective arguments. No doubt and it's really a matter of process. Now, I have a statutory duty and my remarks now are addressed to Mr Clarke and Mr Burken, I have a statutory duty, when both parties are present, to give you an opportunity to try to resolve matters by agreement. You have no obligation to do so but I have a legal obligation to give you the opportunity."

"Conciliation is not about finding out who's right and who's wrong. Conciliation is about finding a solution that everybody can live with. So, I'm sure you've had discussions already and for whatever reasons those discussions haven't resolved the matter but if you would like, despite the late start, if you would like a short opportunity this morning to discuss settlement, I'm happy to give you that opportunity before we get into the submissions and the evidence. What concerns me about this application is this; that in respect of one fairly substantial part of the application it deals with whether certain charges should or should not be included in the budget and those charges are from the operator's point of view. Those charges are less than they would otherwise be because of economies of scale. From the residents' point of view they don't want to pay the charges but what occurred to me when - I haven't seen the documents in this for a couple of weeks and I had a brief opportunity to review the documents that each of you submitted, but what occurred to me when I was reviewing those documents was this. What if the Tribunal took the view that the charges ought not to be included in the budget. Let's say the residents' argument is successful, and if the reason for that was that the operator could not establish the necessary nexus between the amount expended and the service provided. What do you think is going to be the outcome of that?"

"It will be one of two things. Either a service that is withdrawn or alternatively a service that is continued to be provided but the operator may make the nexus very clear on the budget by engaging necessary staff to ensure that everything those people do is attributable to services for Pelican Waters Retirement Village and in doing so the economies of scale may be lost. So what I'm suggesting to you is that there's a possibility here that everybody loses. Now, you'll have a win for the day but a long term loss and that's what I would be very anxious to prevent if I was appearing for one of the parties. I think that's what might focus your minds on trying to come up with a solution. Now, I think, Mr Burken, correct me if I'm wrong, I think there are only two issues that remain in dispute here. One is the insurance issue and the other is the budgetary charges that you're disputing. If you were able to reach agreement on the budget issues I feel that the issues relating to insurance could be dealt with as a discrete and separate item and that's not a difficult matter. It's a very clear matter and the legal argument on it should not be very complicated."

"So what I'm suggesting, I might be quite wrong in that. What I'm suggesting to you is this, if you had a short opportunity right now to discuss the matter privately and to see if you can up with an agreement. I could make orders to give effect to that agreement and that way the matter is resolved, if you can't do that we need to go ahead with the hearing today. The question is; whether each of you are fully authorised by the people you represent to enter into such an agreement."

Jones looked across at Jack. "Yes, Mr Jones, good morning. I'm authorised to represent the residents and I cite the minutes of the meeting of 25th May, residents' meeting, that's attachment M in the Application documents, and attachment Y1, minutes of the 3rd August, residents' meeting and also I submit minutes of a residents' committee meeting held last Thursday which does again endorse my authorisation to speak and represent the residents."

Jones enquired. "Does that give you authority to negotiate on their behalf?"

Jack responded. "It gives me authority to negotiate initially, and we have a quorum of the committee here and I can call a quorum out and in no time at all they would make a decision."

To which Jones responded. "Mmm."

"We have discussed the possibility." Jack added.

The Member then asked, "Yes, and are you willing to enter into those discussions with Mr Burken?"

Jack replied that he was and then Jones looked toward Burken and asked, "Are you authorised to" and before he could finish the sentence Burken jumped in and said "I am".

Jones continued, "to represent the owner? Mr Clarke, what I think should be done is this; a negotiation won't work, now let me re-phrase that. The more people involved in a negotiation the less likely it is to succeed, if you've got two people discussing something it's fairly - it's much more easy to reach an agreement than if one of them is discussing something and the other one is storing up information and taking it back to be discussed in another committee. So, before you go and talk to Mr Burken what you need is the full authority of the residents to allow you to make a deal on their behalf that is binding and you need that full authority. Because people who are outside that negotiation are not aware of what's happened in the process and therefore, may inadvertently or sometimes deliberately scuttle a deal that could be done otherwise. So, are you able to get authority right now?"

Jack's response was, "I can, I can get it right now if I can read from these minutes –".

The Member uttered an, "Mmm."

And Jack continued, "the last two paragraphs, there was a discussion regarding what compromises would be acceptable today if one was offered. It was endorsed by all present that Jack Clarke of Unit 88 Pelican Waters Village is authorised to act on behalf of the residents at the CTTT hearing in respect of the Hearing to be held on the 8th November 2010."

This seemed to satisfy Jones because he then said, "All right, I think you've got the authority unless somebody jumps up and grabs you before you get to the door."

Jack was starting to gain a little confidence in his handling of things to date so he continued. "I'll just ask the members of the committee present or any resident here if anyone wishes to object to what I just read out".

There was a strong, "No objection" from the residents.

Jones responded, "O.K.. Look, while you're doing that I'm going to refresh- review, I'll review the documentation that you're going to be relying on. Is there a place, do you know, that Mr Burken and Mr Clarke could go to privately consider their negotiations?"

Jack advised that Room 147, one of the motel rooms had been set aside for such a purpose.

Jones then said, "O.K.. Maximum half an hour gentlemen, maximum half an hour if you can't do it in that time we need to get going with the hearing. But try and get something on paper with your signature on it".

"If you can do that I'll do the rest. Now everybody else here if these people are going to take maybe ten minutes, maybe half an hour we don't know, they'll be back in at least by 11 o'clock. If you want to sit there I'm happy for you to do that. I'll turn the tape recorder off, or if you want to go outside for a little while by all means do that".

As Jack rose to leave the Hearing room with Pierce Burken he wondered to himself why the Senior Tribunal Member had not required the same degree of proof that Burken had authority to speak and negotiate on behalf of Dollarvill that had been required of himself.

The two men went along the corridor to room 147 which was nearby and entered. It was a little larger than a typical motel room; as well as the sleeping facilities there was a small lounge area with three lounge chairs and a dining area with a table and four chairs. Both sat opposite each other at the table and each placed their folders in front of themselves. Jack commenced by saying, "Ok Pierce, is there anything we can do to resolve this matter?"

Burken replied that the only concession he could offer was as previously and that was a reduction of $994 in the corporate recharge line item.

Jack countered that the residents had already considered that offer and rejected it; was there anything else on the table that he could accept on behalf of the residents. Burken replied that there was not. Jack then tried to open a discussion along the lines of that there was a lot of new information in Dollarvill's response, particularly in respect to corporate recharge and if that information had been forthcoming to the Residents Committee right at the commencement of the budget negotiations then they possibly would not be in the situation that they now found themselves. He then addressed the issue of insurance and said that there were a number of items covered in the evidenced insurance policy which the residents were unwilling to cover the cost of as they were well outside the items that needed to be insured as defined in the Retirement Village Act.

Burken then advised that Dollarvill would be seeking orders from the CTTT that the budget as presented to the residents be enforced. Jack responded with, "Ok, let's go back in and tell Mr Jones that we are unable to reach a compromise and request the Hearing to proceed. The majority of residents attending the Hearing had come out of the Hearing room and were standing around talking in small groups in the corridor, when they saw Clarke and Burken emerge from room 147 they started to file back in to where Jones was still sitting at his table reading through the paperwork.

Jones did not appear surprised when he saw Clarke and Burken return after such a short time. When everyone was seated Jones looked towards Jack and enquired, "Well Mr Clarke, were you able to reach any sort of agreement?" To which Jack replied that they had not.

"O.K., let's get this Hearing underway".

Chapter 7

The CTTT Hearing – Part 2.

Senior Tribunal Member, Jeff Jones, "O.K., you ready, Mr Burken?"

"Yes" replied Burken.

Jones, "Mr Clarke, are you ready"?

Jack answered with a firm "Yes".

Jones addressed Burken, "O.K. Mr Burken, I forgot to ask are you a legal practitioner or not?"

Burken responded somewhat surprised, "Me, no, my brother is".

Jones appeared to take Burken's reply in his stride, "O.K., O.K.. I'll take a few minutes to explain the procedure that we're going to adopt. This is a fairly unusual matter in that we have an application and a cross application and they're both essentially raising the same issues. I think that the way that we should proceed is for each of you to be given a short opportunity perhaps five minutes to give an outline of your case. Where you're going to go with it, whether you're going to be calling witnesses, who they are so that I can get some idea of how long we're going to need to allocate to the parties. Then I think it should be Mr Clarke who speaks first to the documents that he's provided. Are you going to be calling witnesses, Mr Clarke?"

Jack gave a firm, "No".

Jones, "O.K.. So, you'll be referring to the documents that have been filed with the Tribunal. Just on that point I hope everybody's got their mobile phones turned off. I usually turn mine off but I am deliberately leaving it on today because I'm still hopeful that the file's going to turn up at some stage and the courier might ring me so, if you don't mind, I will leave it on for that purpose. So, Mr Clarke, you'll have the opportunity to make your submissions first. Mr Burken, I'll ask you to listen without comment or interruption. If you wish you can take notes and when Mr Clarke is finished you will be given an opportunity to reply. Will you be calling witnesses?"

"No" Burken replied.

Jones, "No, O.K.. So, both sides have been very well documented with this so I don't think there's going to be any difficulty in dealing with the matter in the time that we've got available. I propose that after your introductions that Mr Clarke is given an hour to talk. If he needs more time after that I consider how much more time should be given and then we'll see our way forward from there. So, I'm going to give you approximately the same amount of time to speak. After Mr Burken's finished his submissions, Mr Clarke you'll get a very short opportunity of reply. That's the plan for today. We will break for lunch at some stage. I'm not going to tell you just exactly when that's going to be because it will be at a convenient time during the proceedings. Now, so do you understand the procedure, Mr Clarke?"

Jack replied, "Yes, I believe so".

Jones, "And do you, Mr Burken?"

Burken also answered "Yes".

Jones, "And are you both ready to go ahead with the matter, you've got all of your documentation with you today?"

Both Jack and Burken responded that they were.

Jones then went on, "You don't need to adjourn the matter for any purpose. O.K.. I'll ask you both to take an affirmation to tell the truth".

Both Jack and Burken affirmed that they would tell the truth.

Jones then seemed to go off on another tack when he said, "O.K.. Well, just - I don't know if we even need to do, do you want to do a small, a brief outline of where you're going with it or do you want the documents to speak for themselves?"

Jack who was a little nervous thought to himself, "well here we go Jack give it your best shot". Then he said to Jones, "The documents speak for themselves. I'd just like to commence by saying that I have absolutely no legal training. I have not appeared before a Tribunal before this. I therefore seek your indulgence in respect of my ignorance in this matter".

Without hesitation Jones answered the request, "Mr Clarke, we deal with 60,000 cases a year in the Tribunal, 120,000 parties and nearly all of them are in exactly the same shoes. That's what the Tribunal's for so I have some obligations to explain legal issues to you and give you an opportunity to make your submissions in relation to those issues. I have no obligation to give you advice in any way nor will I do so because in doing so it would be prejudicial to the other side. O.K.. Mr Burken, do you wish to give a short outline or are you happy with your documentation in that regard?"

Burken replied, "As you stated both sides have provided comprehensive folders unless the residents or Mr Clarke wants to go and expand on any of those items".

Jones, "O.K., well I'll just - Mr Clarke is going to speak to his document but I just thought you might've wanted to give me a brief overview of where you're going with it. I have read your documents but not today. O.K., that's a week or two ago".

Burken, "O.K.".

Jack took a deep breath and commenced, "The first issue I'd like to address is the name of the respondent. The initial application Dollarvill Limited and our application both name Dollarvill Limited as the operator. There was a letter dated 28 July 2010 from the CTTT advising that Dollarvill were requesting that the name of the operator be changed to the Highland Investment Pty Limited. We have not received any communications to advise that the CTTT has agreed to that request. In our letter of 3rd August to Dollarvill, attachment X8, we did not object to the change in name in respect of Dollarvill's application however, the application on behalf of the residents cites

Dollarvill Limited as the respondent. We contend that the application should proceed in the name of Dollarvill Limited as all correspondence, advertising, budgets, letters, publications, information are in the name Dollarvill Limited. We would suggest that Dollarvill Limited are seeking to distance themselves from this hearing by the use of one of its subsidiary companies, and if this Tribunal were to find against the Highland Investment Company Pty Limited, Dollarvill Limited would not have to comply with that part of the legislation that requires all such findings to be reported in their disclosure statements".

Jones appeared a little taken back by Jack's attack and in an effort to regain control of the proceedings he responded, "Well, Mr Clarke, I think that it's not going to be helpful by making pejorative statements of that nature. I think it is an important issue to identify the correct naming of the respondent but to put improper motives on that issues I think is unhelpful. But I take the point, I've already asked Mr Burken that informally before the hearing started but I'm happy to follow that up for you now. Before I do that what's on the contracts that all the residents have signed. Have they signed a contract with Dollarvill?"

Jack replied, "Pelican Waters Village Pty Limited".

Jones, "Well, isn't that the name of the respondent? Shouldn't that be the correct party?"

Jack, "Well it's now operated by Highland, it changed recently".

Jones, "Mmm and Mr Burken informs me this morning that one or both of the companies is in the process of being taken over by a company called Landbuild. So, I don't know, perhaps Mr Burken can give us some information but before I ask him to respond to that issue I'll just have a look at the contracts themselves.

Burken tried to be helpful by advising, "I think it's tab 3 or 4".

After Jones had a quick look at the lease documents he said, "Its Pelican Waters Village Pty Limited is the contracting party. So it would appear to me that, unless there's some really good reason to change that, the respondent should be Pelican Waters Village Pty Limited".

Burken jumped in, "Can I just respond to –".

Jones, "Yes".

Burken commenced, "What Dollarvill - over a period of time has acquired a number of different companies and during that course of time we've let those, like Pelican Waters Pty Limited, stay. A decision was made a while back as to have one company run all our subsidiaries. The reason for that is; it is very difficult and costly for us to run all these different companies. So we did start the process, I'll say start the process of converting all the companies into Highland Investments and you are right, Mr Clarke, saying that it hasn't gone to ACCC and the reason for that is during the merger or acquisition of Landbuild all of those processes had to be ceased until the merger was finished. I've spoken to Landbuild on that and once this merger is complete we intend to go back to Highland Investments. That is the reason why it altered them.

Jones then trying to clarify the matter asked, "Well, what's happened to Pelican Waters Village Pty Limited?"

Burken responded, "It's still there we want to roll it into Highland Investments".

Adopting a school Master attitude Jones said, "Well, you need to use terms that have some legal meaning "rolling into" I don't understand what you mean by that term".

Burken, "So it can be re-named Highland Investments".

Jones, "So, it's just a re-naming of the company?"

Burken, "of the company".

Jones, "Of Pelican Waters Village Pty Limited to Highland?"

Burken, "Highland Investments".

Jones, "Has that happened in regard to this one or not?"

Burken, "At the commencement of this procedure it had, I don't believe it's been formalised though".

Jones, "So, is it or isn't it?"

Burken, "Well because as I set out, proceedings were stopped due to the merger that came through".

Jones, "So, the registered company is in the name of Pelican Waters Village Pty Limited?"

Burken, "Yes, it is Pelican Waters, you're correct".

Jones, "O.K.. So, Dollarvill Pty Limited".

Burken, "It's Dollarvill Limited".

Jones, "Dollarvill Limited is it?"

Burken, "A listed company on the stock exchange".

Jones, "So what role does that company have?"

Burken, "It's just a - doesn't own the asset that we're talking about today".

Jones, "Does it own Pelican Waters Village, all the shares from Pelican Waters Village?"

Burken, "Yes".

Jones, "O.K., so then Pelican Waters Village would appear to be a subsidiary of Dollarvill Limited and Dollarvill Limited may or may not be in the process of being taken over by Landbuild but that's really irrelevant to the matters today".

Jack, "I agree"

The Tribunal Member in summing up the situation said, "So the respondent should be, in my view, Pelican Waters Village Pty Limited".

Burken, "We have no problem with that".

Jones, "O.K. So I'll make a - I'll make a procedural order that the operator's name on both files is amended to Pelican Waters Village Pty Limited and that order is made by consent of the parties. Thanks, Mr Clarke, go ahead please".

Jack took a deep breath and commenced, "Well there are two issues corporate re-charge or management fee and insurance. The budget was rejected on 25th May unanimously by the residents of Pelican Waters Village because of those two issues and another issue at the time. The issues are well documented in our submission, as to the reasons for this, but I'd go a little further regarding the non-acceptance and the rise in the current charges. We have never said that the rise of 4.4 per cent on current charge for the year 2010/11 was excessive. The reason for refusing to agree to the rise was that it seemed the correct thing to do considering the fact that we intended to reject the budget because of our objections to insurance and the corporate recharge. Regarding insurance, we do not necessarily consider the sum of $23,100.00 necessary excessive for the insurance. The question is should the residents be paying for insurance at all."

"We're concerned that there is a total lack of transparency on Dollarvill's part as far as the insurance policy covering the village is concerned. We are not even aware of which company the policy is with. We are aware that leases say that the recurrent charges can be used to cover insurance costs and that the Act says that insurance can be met from a recurrent charge if approved by the residents; however we do not know just what is being insured. Residents feel that the insurance taken out for the village offers them little or no protection as they are lessees. They do not own any property nor do they have any insurable interests in the village. Residents are not protected by the public liability coverage in the village insurance. We are puzzled at the inclusion of the sample standalone policy contained in Dollarvill's response and we have never requested that the village be insured separately from Dollarvill's other villages. If that sample policy is a fair comparison with the actual cover Dollarvill has arranged for Pelican Waters Village it would seem that we are expected to cover a number of risks which do not apply to Pelican Waters Village. We hold little or no cash on the premises nor cash in transit, we have no works of art or antiques. We see no point in insuring against murder or suicide. It seems to that we are also insuring Dollarvill against loss of profits and covering executive salaries 100 per cent for three years. Even if the whole village was razed to the ground we do not believe that Dollarvill would suffer a loss of profit. They would still have ingoing contributions some $20 million worth invested and how would such catastrophic event affect the employment and salaries of executive staff."

"Dollarvill themselves quote section 100, sub section 2, of the Act which states that the operator is required to hold insurance covering a) damage, b) cost incidental to the re-instatement or replacement of the insured buildings c) public liability and d) provides for the re-instatement of property to its condition when new. No mention is made of insurance against loss of profits, safeguarding executive salaries or any other risks that our insurance policy apparently covers. We would suggest that if residents are expected to cover insurance costs then the liability should be limited to the essentials mentioned in section 100, sub section 2 of the Act. We contend that the insurance cover of the village is largely for Dollarvill's benefit and as such should be at their cost not ours. For the corporate re-charge the information now"

At this point Jones cut in with, "Sorry, just before you go on to that, Mr Clarke, let me ask you how are you aware that the issues that you raise; cash on the premises, works of art, murder and suicide, loss of profits how are you aware that those risks are insured?

Jack responded, "Attachment A to Mr Burken's witness statement is a quotation from an Insurance Broker and they list all these things. It's a separate insurance quote for insurance Pelican Waters Village and all of these things are listed in it.

Jones, "Sorry go on. Is that, that's the only document you're relying on in regard to that?"

Jack, "In regard to those bits and pieces."

Jones, "O.K., yes."

Jack continued, "Now, the corporate recharge. The information now provided was whilst illuminating does not change our view that we are not liable to pay the charges re the corporate recharge. Our view is simple; each year we pay through the current charges and agreed cost for the delivery of general services in our village. At no time prior Dollarvill's ownership had it been suggested that we were liable to pay additional funds to meet head office's costs incurred by the delivery of general service to our residents by our onsite staff. We reject entirely that we have any liability for such costs and we have already agreed and consent to the delivery of such services. Corporate re-charge was introduced by Dollarvill's first budget for the village for the year ending June 2008 and despite claims to the contrary Dollarvill have steadfastly avoided giving us any details as to what it covers. We were given a percentage breakdown for the 2008/09 budget but only with persistent urging from the committee. Initially this year the percentage breakdown was all the information provided. With the new requirements under the Act we were finally able to gain some insight into just what we were paying for, but again, only after repeated requests from the committee to do that."

"The cost of corporate recharge of $28,594 is a concern to the residents. It represents seven per cent of total budget. Dollarvill say that the $28,594 they wish to bill the village for this year amounts to only $230 per unit. However, in the annexure they claim for administration, finance and IT they charge the village only 25 per cent of the actual cost thereof. Now, if this is so then the actual cost per unit rising to $860. If you multiply this by the 3108 independent living units that they have in all of their villages you'll arrive at the total sum $2.7 million. This is a conservative estimate as many villages are larger and have more staff per units than Pelican Waters Village. We find it hard to believe that the department dealing with retirement villages at Dollarvill's head office really costs $2.7 million to run on a yearly basis. Therefore, we query our share of those costs."

"We are especially concerned that when multiplying the number of staff Dollarvill say are involved in their stated costs per hour we arrive at an annual sum of only 1.5 million, a vastly lower figure. On reviewing Dollarvill's annexure "Corporate Recharge" the committee was concerned to see that many of facilities we are paying for have little or nothing to do with daily running of the village they are operational costs that should be borne by Dollarvill. Residents appreciate the time, effort and many skills necessary to efficiently run a village such as ours and have no quarrel with the way it is currently managed. We also understand that on occasion the manager will require some input from head office by way of advice or assistance. However, we already pay for the manager's services and that of her assistant through our recurrent charges and see no reason why we should have to pay for head office input and that equals paying twice for the one action."

"Every business has operating costs and it is most unfair we feel for Dollarvill to defray those costs by imposing a corporate recharge on residents who are already paying for the daily running costs of the village. Corporate recharges were included in our annual budget by Dollarvill upon them becoming the operator of the village. From the time we were exposed to the expression we have pondered as to its meaning. Now having the information disclosed by the respondent it is apparent that this title has been carefully chosen in order to not disclose the nature of the charges which were to be included in the single line item of the budget. It also explains the reluctance of Dollarvill to clarify the detail of how this item was calculated. The only clue we had was the word "recharge". If something is recharged it means that it is being charged again. That is, more than once. That gives credence to your claim that many of the present list items are additional charges for service which have been agreed to and paid for under the current charges contained in the annual budget. We note also that Dollarvill in their previous advice was that we would not be required to pay for the annual audit. The residents of Pelican Waters Village respectfully request that insurance and corporate recharge should be excluded from the budget."

Jones, "Thanks Mr Clarke. Anything else, Mr Clarke, at this stage?"

Jack responded, "No, that's the end of it".

Jones, "O.K., well that's quick. Mr Burken are you ready to".

Burken quickly answered, "Yes".

"OK, go ahead Mr Burken". Jones invited.

Burken, "Thank you, Mr Clarke, I appreciate the time and effort that the residents put behind this. We consider insurance –".

Jones cut in, "Mr Burken, you're talking to me".

Burken, "Sorry".

Jones, "O.K., not Mr Clarke, with the greatest respect".

This set Burken back a little then he commenced, "All right, we consider insurance and corporate recharge necessary costs to ensure proper running of the village. In particular the items that are raised by Mr Clarke in terms of insurance and what they believe they should or shouldn't pay their contracts state they need to cover "*Insurance premiums payable by the lessor in respect of all buildings, fittings, fixtures of Pelican Waters Village to the full insurable re-statable value.*" Mr Clarke has outlined a few line items which is the cash on premises, the cash in transit, unfortunately the nature of the business is that you need to cover those areas under your insurance, particularly cash in transit. It's a risk and it's a very small cost to the organisation. Death on premises, unfortunately again, you need to cover that we have had some incidents recently where that has occurred and the village is required to have insurance in that area".

Jones then cut in, "Sorry, just on that point".

Burken, "Yes".

Jones, "I don't think I have a copy of the contract in front of me but do you say that the contract, just read that little provision in the contract that deals with the insurance if you wouldn't mind".

Not seeming to understand the request Burken asked, "From the residents' budget?".

Jones, "No, no, in the contract itself, the requirement to - for the residents - the undertaking by the residents in the contract to pay for insurance. What does that say?".

Burken, "It says all insurance premiums payable by the lessor in respect of all buildings, fittings, fixtures of Pelican Waters Village for their full insurable re-statable value".

Jones, "But that's nothing to do with cash in transit is it?"

Burken, "Section, another section of it".

Jones, "O.K.".

Burken, "Reasonable costs inclusive of wages, superannuation, pension payments, workers compensation insurance, management control and administration of Pelican Waters Village which does cover that".

Jones, "So you say that's included?"

Burken, "Yes".

Jones, "All right. Yes, go on".

Burken, "I'm not quite understanding why Mr Clarke would bring up the point if the village did unfortunately did burn to the ground the company would be fully re-instated, it would take three to five years to re-build the village and bring it up to level. We've got insurance in place to insure that residents have accommodation during the re-building of the village. Which is a necessary part of insurance and so I'm not quite sure why that was brought up this morning".

Jones, "So, have you provided copies of the insurance policies showing what is covered to the residents?"

Burken, "We obtain our insurance from a broker and that broker buys on behalf of the group for us to individually break that down per village, per unit is very difficult for us to do".

Jones getting a little impatient, "No, no, I'm not asking you to break it down per village, per unit, I'm asking whether the residents of this village are advised in writing at any time of what risks are, in fact, insured?"

Burken, "By their contracts when they come in, but not whilst they're residents there we do not show the ongoing"

Jones again cut in, "So, they have to take it on trust that what you've insured or what your broker has covered is dealt with under the contract. That's what you're saying?"

Burken, "Yes".

Jones, "And they're saying we're not taking it on trust, we want you to prove to us that you have not exceeded your - the provisions of the contract or section 100. That's essentially the case, so they don't know nor can they know whether you've insured your sailing boat in the lagoon or the managing director's Lamborghini, they simply have no knowledge of what risks are covered by the insurance that you're asking them to pay for".

Burken continued, "Not written, no. On that point, say for example, workers compensation; now workers compensation is bundled in with our general insurance. Now the village has had a number of claims of workers compensation, has had three in the last five years. We've never broken that down and individually back to residents for that insurance component, we've continued to approve it as a general insurance cost. So, I suppose its swings and roundabouts. We don't provide all the full details and their covering in there, unless they ask for it and no one has asked for it until today".

Jones, "Well, there's been a certain amount of disquiet on the issues since last May; people have said we're not going to pay it. I would've thought that it would be absolutely in your interests to give them chapter and verse on what's covered. It might, for example, be considerable enlightenment for the residents to know that they will have somewhere else to live if the place burns to the ground".

Burken, "Mr Jones, I believe they were given that information".

Jones questioned, "When and how?"

Burken, "I don't really - I don't know the exact date, I don't have the exact date in front of me."

JONES: How was it given?

Burken, "I understand it was provided to the office there for them to read".

Jones, "O.K., so what you can say to me is that the residents have not been given any detail of the risks covered under the insurance for which they are being asked to pay. Is that what you're?"

Burken cut in, "No, I don't - I believe they have been provided the details that they requested".

Jones asked, "So, you tell me how they were provided?"

Floundering a little Burken replied, "O.K., I can't right now so"

Jones, "So, there is no evidence that the residents have been provided with this information".

Burken, "I was lead to believe that they have been provided with it".

Jones, "O.K. See, Mr Burken, what I'm concerned about here; there are a few things that Mr Clarke said that doesn't worry me. I don't care whether the residents know who your insurance company is or not. I don't even know who my own insurance company is, you don't need to know until you need to know - make a claim and in any event the residents are not going to make a claim".

The mobile phone on Jones's table started to ring. "Excuse me, this may be what I'm waiting for". Jones takes a call on his mobile phone regarding the courier who is delivering his files. "O.K., that file is on its way".

"Sorry, I was saying that it doesn't matter, in my view, that the residents don't know who your insurance company is. Because they're never going to have to fill out the insurance policy, what they do need to know is a) that there is insurance in place b) what it covers because goodness me, we're being asked to pay $28,500 for this insurance and they would like to know just what - that you have, in fact fulfilled, when I say "you" I don't mean you personally I meant the operator, has fulfilled its legal and contractual obligations. The problem is that they've got no way of knowing. They can't get the documents out of you, they've got no access to the broker so the only person or the only organisation that can do anything about this is the operator of the village who can get a copy of the policy and say, there you are folks that's what we're paying $28,500 for. That hasn't been done has it?"

Jack thought to himself that the Senior Tribunal Member had got the amounts of $28,500 for corporate recharge and the correct amount relating to insurance of $23,100 mixed up.

Burken, "I was lead to believe it had been done. For the residents then to quote from it clearly they must have seen the document".

Quite firmly Jones responded, "No, no, Mr Clarke was not quoting from that, he was quoting from an attachment to a statement filed by you".

Burken tried to extradite himself from the situation he found himself in with, "I was under the impression that the residents were aware of the items covered by the policy as they were known to me, yes".

Jones, "Mmm. All right, I've interrupted you, - you were about to go onto the corporate recharge issue but I just--"

Burken, "No, I was still on the--"

Jones, "Mmm?"

Burken, "--I was still on the insurance".

Jones, "Still on the insurance issue, O.K. All right, just continue on with that".

Burken, "O.K., in terms of the insurance the residents have claimed that there's ambiguity with the word "*may*" insurance "*may*" fund, operators are entitled to on charge insurance costs as the Act does not state operators must fund insurance. So we're stating under the Act we're following it, and the insurance costs, pertaining to that village is being charged on and we believe there's no ambiguity in there. The reasonableness of the charge, the proposed budget allocates $23,100 to the insurance item. The insurances held for the village is covered in the head policy or on behalf of the village by Dollarvill relates to the items covered in section 100 of the Act. Specifically the amount payable in respect of the village in Dollarvill's portfolio total insurance. This is where the difficulties, Mr Jones comes through because it is combined in through the group".

"The allocation of insurance between the various portfolios is calculated by using a formula and that is the village value divided by the total value of the group equals the insurance premium."

Jones, "I don't think Mr Clarke's disputing that. I think that he's saying that if we have to pay the insurance, the formula that's been calculated on is good enough for us. I don't want to put words in your mouth".

Jack tried to clarify the residents position, "We're not querying $23,100 costs per se, we're agreeing that we have to pay it".

Jones, "Right. O.K.".

Burken, "We were lead to believe you didn't want to pay any insurance whatsoever".

Jones, "Well, they've refused the insurance for the reason that they've explained".

Burken, "Well, I'm sorry I just want clarification on it. My understanding was that they believe they're tenants therefore being tenants they don't pay any insurance. That was the argument that they put forward twice".

Jones, "Mmm. O.K.. But I think the reasonableness of the way that you've calculated it is not in issue. They're not saying that the formula that has been used is an unreasonable method of doing it".

Burken, "Right".

Jones, "So, I don't need to inquire into that unless you particularly want to. I know you've provided documentation on it but I don't need to inquire into that because Mr Clarke is not saying that the method of calculation is flawed in any way. Do you say that reasonableness is a criteria that must be applied in any event. You mentioned reasonableness of the charges".

Burken, "Correct".

Jones, "Do you say that reasonableness of the charges is one of the criteria that I need to examine?"

Burken, "In particular with insurance".

Jones, "And where does that arise?".

Burken, "The reasonableness of our calculation and the--"

He was cut off by Jones with, "No, no the reasonableness of the amount being charged, where does that arise? Do you say that arises somewhere under the contract or under the legislation?".

Burken, "Under the Act is says that when you provide the insurance for it and we are reasonably applying it, does that answer your question".

Jones, "O.K., well not exactly, what - I'm trying to draw a distinction between is the way in which you've calculated how much should be attributed to Pelican Waters out of - let's say the total insurance contract cost your company $100,000 and you've come up with a formula that allocated $21,000 I think for the insurance $21,000 to Pelican Waters. Now they're not saying that there is any unreasonableness in the way that it has been apportioned, what they're saying is that there is unreasonableness in the inclusion of insurance for which they should not be held liable. They have argued that on the basis that they don't have any benefit from any of the insurance and I think Mr Clarke's putting that argument to me which I think is a very difficult argument to give full value to because of the statutory provisions and because of the contractual provisions. I think that it seems pretty apparent to me and I don't want to appear as though I'm prejudging this, but I think it's pretty apparent to me that the residents are going to be up for the insurance as set out under the Act and as set out under the contract".

"What I have difficulty with is the inclusion in that global sum, in that $100,000, of amounts that the residents have no way of knowing where it came from. What risk is insured, how is it attributable to; how do the residents of Pelican Waters Village get any benefit of that. I facetiously mentioned the insurance on the boat parked out on the lagoon. Now let's say, for example, that was the case. We've got the big cruiser out on the lagoon and there's ten thousand bucks worth of insurance on it and that's being somehow fed back into the $100,000. Now, that's attributing a very dishonest motive to the respondent and I don't want to do that, I'm using it as an illustration only. O.K.? But the difficulty is that the residents at no time have an opportunity to excise, to know about that risk that's being insured, and to excise that from the budgeted insurance".

"So, I guess what I'm thinking is this; that some insurance seems to me pretty obviously an obligation on the residents. Mr Clarke's shaking his head and he'll have a chance to disagree with me on that in due course. But it seems to me that every resident has signed a contract to that effect and the law provides that that's O.K. to sign such a contract. But the difficulty I see is in the residents being able to know what it is that they are paying for so that they can take meaningful objection to it. So, in circumstances where there is no way of knowing whether or not the insurance component complies with the Act and complies with the contract why should the residents pass it?".

Burken, 'Could I field a response to this, Mr Jones?".

Jones, "Yes, please".

Burken, "Firstly, I was under the assumption they had received a breakdown. To the best of our knowledge breaking it down under a group policy which, if that isn't the case, we can resolve that. That's the first one. You're talking about the reasonableness of it, we divided it, as I said, with a formula that breaks down the cost of the village compared to the total sum of the company providing insurance for the - and I can provide that formula which is the pack that was provided on page 9 of tab 1. I'd also like to just--".

Jones, "I've now got the paperwork so I'll just grab that out. I've got all those there. So you're referring to?".

Burken, "It was tab 1 and I was referring to page 9 and 8".

Jones, "Right, just give me a moment please".

"68 and 69", said Burken trying to be helpful.

Jones, "Yes".

Burken, "Clauses 68 and 69 gave a breakdown of formula used to calculate the amount of insurance charged for each village".

Burken, "That's how we reasonably calculate the charge back to the residents. We've also made mention that because we are buying in bulk if there's any savings we do pass those onto the residents and as the residents are aware the insurance costs in 2007 was $27,608 again through management, negotiating powers we are able to bring that cost down substantially and pass the savings onto residents. Again, we're applying reasonable cross benefits back to the residents. Another point there, Mr Jones, is - you're saying breaking down the individual items of insurance. With industrial special risk you buy insurance with packages contained and it's not unfortunately often up to us to break down individually why it is within that insurance".

Jones was not having any of the spin that was being floated, he challenged Burken, "That's not what I'm talking about at all. I don't know whether I've explained this point and I'm putting the point that Mr Clarke has put to me. I don't need to see how many dollars are being charged to the respondent in respect of the risks associated with cash in transit, couldn't care less. What I am caring about is what risks are covered under that policy and whether or not they come within the provisions of the contract. That's the issue".

Burken, "O.K.".

Jones continued, "And there is no evidence that's been provided on that issue as far as I can tell".

Burken, "O.K.".

Jones, "So, the drop from $27,600 to $23,100 was an economy of scale".

Burken, "Plus buying through larger insurance companies".

Jones, "And the increase - I guess the only reason I've mentioned this, Mr Burken, is that I don't want you to - I don't like having the wool pulled over my eyes and I think that when you say that something is not dissimilar but there's a 15 per cent difference I think that is significant and I think it would've been more appropriate to say this year there is a 15 per cent difference because of increased costs for workers comp or something of that nature if that's the actual cause of it. That's the reason I pointed out that section to you".

Burken, "All right, O.K.".

Jones, "Now, I've interrupted you so please continue".

Burken, "When the village was a standalone village we provided - we got some quotes from insurers and we covered the insurance adequately for the village, we were lead to believe was $48,851.98. Again through our purchasing power passing on costs we believe are acting in the best interests of the residents".

Jones, "Mmm, and this is the point I raised with you at the start before I sent you off to conciliation that the downside risk for the residents is that the operator goes away and gets standalone insurance for $48,000 and charges it back to the residents. That's the downside risk for them in running this sort of argument. O.K.. We're aware of that issue, thanks, Mr Burken".

Burken continued, "That's all for insurance from us. Corporate recharge, in the proposed budget we put in line corporate recharge. Corporate recharge as the residents have indicated covers a number of areas of expertise that we provide to the village and those costs have been broken down in a percentage basis and in a dollar basis with our submission. We've also drawn our cost basis against strata villages which we run and we've used a medium cost price as opposed to the costs of the market charging back to residence at strata villages.

Again, we believe the costs here are directly related, they're only for the village and the running of the village".

Jones questioned, "Why do you say that?".

Burken, "Why do I say that? Shall I go through each line item that we do cover through that?".

Jones, "Yes, if you wish. Because I think this is the critical point of this whole day".

Burken, "So the corporate recharge in summary is broken down into administration, finance, human resources, information technology. Now the residents have advised me that in past years, many years ago one person covered all of these areas. In my experience I've not come across an individual that can cover all these areas to ensure that the business can be run adequately, not one individual. Administration represents activities at head office pertaining to issue and management of contracts, compliance, government's regulation matters, and other legislative matters reliant to the current operations. Finance represents processing and payments of supplier invoices, again pertaining to the village, building and maintenance of resident records, preparation of monthly financial reports, maintenance and the preparation of village budget, attending to resident queries and other accounting matters".

"Human resources, represents payroll processing, maintaining personal records and attending to staffing matters at the village. Information technology, due to the village's location we've made sure that the village has well established systems for network connected village to global communications which allows us to assist the management of the village and the residents from our head office".

When Burken indicated that information technology assisted in the management of the residents Jack thought to himself, "That would be right, they want to manage the residents rather than have the residents live their lives as individuals".

Burken went on, "I believe the items we've listed here are necessary for the proper administration and management of the village having directly provided to the village and are for the benefit of the residents. The reasonableness of the charge in respect to the residents, they're objection to the quantum does not constitute a legitimate objection to the item of expenditure where it shows the services form part of the general services provided to the village".

"The items form part of the administration management that is the capital under the village contracts. The costs are on the evidence directly associated with delivery of services to the village and the services that are necessarily needed for the administration management of the village as they are not services that can be performed; I stress this, solely by the village manager".

"By centralising Dollarvill's head office this allows significant specialist operation support provided to the village at reasonable cost. It is also the answer to the efficient operation of Dollarvill's portfolio utilising plans of scale for residents. We have calculated in terms of a formula the hours per week for each one of the departments we talk about, administration, HR et cetera, on a flat rate of $36.00 an hour. By using that $36.00 an hour we've applied a formula of the hours per week by a particular individual or a department to assist the village. There is a table there including pages 12 and 13 in terms of calculations. The residents have commented that they've been asking for this information and not received it. In my experience in the village we provided the break down for the last three years, and I've been individually there for every one of those years and they did get that and I can go back and--"

Jones cut in, "So why did you pick on an hourly wage of $36.00 an hour".

Burken was not ready for the question and stuttered, "Because if you go - ". Chaplin, sitting on Burken's right seeing that Burken was having problems quietly prompted him with something about strata.

Burken then went on, "We draw comparison to our villages that are run by strata and the strata functions covers a lot of administration and management. The company we're talking about is Right and Duncan and their fees per individual covering that ranges - for accounting staff their hourly rate is $77.00 per hour, for administration staff it's $66.00 an hour and it goes up from there".

Jones, "The reason I'm asking is this, it would seem to me again, Mr Clarke is not disputing the way in which the amount has been apportioned he's saying two things I think. I think he's saying two things, firstly he's saying that the service - it has not been demonstrated that the services for which a charge is being made provide a benefit to the residents of this village and secondly, there is no evidence at all that the apportionment is based on actual costs to the operator".

Burken, "Well, we've tried to demonstrate this by breaking down here with the table exactly the hours provided".

Jones, "Yes".

Burken, "And the benefits to the residents to ensure compliance. For example, this year alone dealing with the workers comp claims that we're dealing with right now and individual village managers, no disrespect to them, don't have the skill set to deal with the complex nature of a workers comp claim".

Jones, "When you say - I'm looking at paragraph 95 of your submission now, applying the formula, you've got an actual recharge and adjusted recharge, in this case the same for administration it would seem to me to be an appropriate starting point to say this is what it's cost Dollarvill for administration charges at head office. It cost us $175,000 for the year, $275,000 whatever it is".

Burken, "As a total".

Jones, "As a total for charges that can be attributed to the various villages that you're administering and then you attribute those charges on some sort of formula like the one that you've used. I don't have a problem with the formula. What I have a problem with is knowing firstly; whether the charges come within the definition under the regulations and secondly, what is the actual amount incurred. What the actual cost is to the operation. So we're not reimbursing - you call it a corporate recharge, we're not trying to apply a charge to reimburse for a fictitious cost, we're trying to attribute an actual cost based on a proportion to these people and you've provided me no evidence at all as far as I'm aware of the actual costs to Dollarvill. You've done it on the basis of a theoretical $36.00 an hour for average charge but if you - it would seem to me that you would need to establish, look we paid out this amount of money for these services, all of these services provided a benefit to the residents of Pelican Waters. They provided benefits to a whole lot of other people as well and we've got to divide those - that cost up. But, there's no connection between what you're allocating in these recurrent charges to what you've actually paid".

Burken, "Well, I'm sorry, I believe that we have broken it down based on the number of staff there, that's at the basis and again we - ".

Jones again interrupted, "So what you would do is - tot up their wages. We've got Mary, Josie, and Adam and their total salary for the year is X number of dollars but that evidence has not been provided to me".

Burken, "There is a method for calculation of corporate recharge, have you seen that?".

Jones, "I've got the method in front in me, yes, but it's based on a fictitious, I say fictitious figure, of $36.00 an hour. What I'm more interested in is whether the people actually that were working for you incurred $36.00 per hour that you're paying that. That's what I'm interested in".

After another prompt from Chaplin, Burken continued, "O.K., so you want the calculation of their hourly running. You just also mentioned there about what is the total cost to the organisation. Now they are a public listed company, it's in the annual report of a figure of 15 million dollars".

Jones, "But that's not what we're talking about here. We're talking about a way of showing the people of Pelican Waters that you've complied with the regulation. The regulation, I'll just take you to the regulation, clause 26 (e). It says there that *"Things that must not be financed are costs associated with the operator's head office or management or administration fees unless,"* and there's the *"unless"*. *"Unless the cost or fees are associated with providing services to residents of the retirement village."* So, you've got a number of provisos there, *"the costs"*. Now, not a fictitious cost, not a cost, an average cost or something *"the actual cost"* and you need to be able to associate the actual costs with the provision of services to residents of the retirement village not sixteen different retirements, these, this retirement village".

Burken tried to cut in, "On that point - ".

Jones, "So that's how you get it within that exculpation under the regulations. If you can't do that then it would seem to me that the preamble to that regulation says you're not allowed to charge it".

Burken, "O.K., and just on the current Act there we are to provide an hour by hour billing but for us to do that we would have to engaged the services of another employee to actually track and record that, which will add costs to it as and per a strata village. So I raised the point with, I've raised this before with the CTTT, saying we are concerned that if you want to apply exact hourly costs we will have to hire more staff to track it and the sort of costs we will pass onto residents".

Jones, "Well, the difficulty I have is being satisfied with establishing that what you're trying to charge in this - as you've calculated it here and you've applied it. We've got - you know $5,364 for administrative charges and $15,727 for finance is that cost that are incurred. Show me your accounts that establish that was a cost that was incurred. See, there's no evidence put on about any of that, Mr Burken, and that's my difficulty here".

Burken again prompted by Chaplin, "There is a statement from Dollarvill in tab 4".

Jones, "Is there, where in tab 4?".

Burken, "Tab 4" indicating on his folder that tabs 4 was towards the end of the response document.

Jones, "O.K., thank you".

Jack cut in with, "Mr Jones, you said I wasn't to interrupt if you hold up your hand I'll shut up, but the information you're dealing with now is supplied in the document for the CTTT. None of this information has ever been given to the residents in order that they could consider the budget".

Jones, "Well once you got it from the - as a result of the directions that would've enabled you to consider your position at least, Mr Clarke".

Jack could not follow Jones's reasoning and considered that as the residents might be in front that he would not enter into a debate with the Senior Tribunal Member.

Jones, "O.K., sorry, I'm looking at a witness statement from - Amam Lam is that right, Mr Burken?".

Burken, "Yes, Mr Jones".

Jones, "O.K., just give me a few minutes with that if you wouldn't mind".

Burken, "Yes".

Jones took a couple of minutes to look over Lam's statement.

Jones, "Yes, thanks Mr Burken, I've had a chance to read that. What do you want to say about it?".

Burken, "Sir, I was just referring to - you were talking about calculation of corporate re-charge how we came to those figures. Mr Lam who's our financial controller and there is his statement and how we break that down and calculate it. And you were drawing to - if you look at page 4 of Mr Lam and section 17 your comments earlier on Mr Jones was, *what is the total number*," if you look at section b there it talks about the 9 employees and then how we divide that up in relating to the village.

Jones, "So, was any of that information provided to the residents at the time the budget was put to them?".

Burken, "We provide a letter to the residents about the proposed budget. We did one at 28 April 2010 this year and at the back of it, it has some attachments and attachment 2 of that letter which would be in your tab C, sorry D and it talks about corporate recharge percentage there".

Jones, "D, did you say?".

Burken, "Yes".

Jones, "Thank you".

Burken, "D, attachment 2, you'll see the back of the correspondence".

Jones, "Yes".

Burken, "In that statement "residents' budget framework" at the top?".

Jones, "Yes, I've got that".

Burken, "O.K., and then on the following page it starts *"proposed annual budget"* there's a total at the top and then a number of categories underneath".

Jones, "And that's provided, all of that is provided you say at the time - that's attached to the proposed budget?".

Burken, "Yes it was sent out to all residents on 28 April 2010".

Jones, "All right".

Burken, "So I hope page 14, number 17 explains the total number of employees engaged at Dollarvill's head office and how they're calculated back to the respective village and then we've applied attachment 2 with proportions in terms of percentages and that's how we've come to the formula. In terms of the residents being aware of it, as we said we have broken it down on the resident budget framework corporate recharge explanations".

Jones, "One of the things, Mr, what's his name, Mr Lam says is at paragraph 13 he says, *"To determine the corporate recharge amount it is necessary to undertake the following process. Calculate the total head office costs referrable to the operation of the retirement village portfolio."* How's that done?".

Burken, "If you go to point 16, *"Calculating total cost of head office and resources this is the sum of"* and then he's broken it down into a number of sections".

Jones, "O.K. but that doesn't answer the question. The total staff who are allocated or identified as being used for the provision of services to the villages. I guess, what, what I'm thinking here, so looking at the IT for example, you've got two full time IT people, is that right?".

Burken, "Yes".

Jones, "So - - "

Burken, "Well one of them is actually, technically, a contractor who is there full time".

Jones, "So what duties do they have that are attributable to operation of the retirement villages and if, and I think the other side of that coin is what duties do they have that are not attributable to the operation of the retirement villages?".

Burken, "Do you want me to explain that to you now?".

Jones, "Yes please, yes, yes".

Burken, 'So, information technology, there are comments in, in the filing but I'll read through it. All villages now have significant levels of technology, computers are the primary form of retention of corporate and resident information".

Jones, "Is this in your documentation?".

Burken, "Yes".

Jones, "Whereabouts is it?".

Burken, "Witness statement 3. On page 5 of my affidavit there".

Jones, "Right. I can read that for myself, do you have anything to add to it?".

Burken, "I believe it covers the ambient of your question".

Jones, "Does it, O.K.. All right, I'll need to have a closer look at that. All right, go on, Mr Burken".

Burken, "Right, where were we Mr Jones?".

Jones trying to lead Burken along the correct way, continued. "I don't know, we're not disputing and I don't think Mr Clarke wants to go into the actual allocation. You've adopted a different criteria for different items within the corporate recharge but I don't think Mr Clarke is taking and he can correct me if I'm wrong, but I don't think he's taking exception to that. So, do you want to talk about the statutory framework for example, in which you are entitled to make these charges?".

Burken, "Would you like me to go through section 4 here, compliance with the Act and regulations".

Jones, "Whatever you want, I'm in your hands".

Burken, "O.K.".

Jones, "The question I had for you before we go to that perhaps and I know the answer to that question, Mr Clarke's answered that question. Go ahead Mr Burken".

Burken, "So our new compliance with the Act and regulations proposed by – proposed - ". Burken was here prompted by Chaplin and continued, "- division 5 part 7 of the Act as the increased, proposed budget under section 112 is to be funded by way of increase of recurrent charges under section 106 of the Act the respondent was required to provide the residents with a copy of the budget and appropriate budget notice of at least sixty days prior to the commencement of the budget. Initially the respondent sought to increase the recurrent charges under section 106 of the Act to meet the budget's increased expenditure by way of non-fixed - increase in recurrent charges that exceeds CPI. The respondent through its head office provided the residents of the village with a copy of the proposed budget, budget notice and a notice of variation of recurrent charges by letter dated 28/10, which we talked about earlier and in 68 prior to the end of the financial year for the village. Annexed and marked "D" is a copy in the file of respondent's letter dated 28 April which we talked just briefly before. After receiving respondent's letter dated 28 April requesting consent to the proposed budget and variation in recurrent charges the residents met, considered and voted on propose budget and variation of recurrent charges in accordance with section 107 and 114 (4) of the Act".

Jack looked at Bob McTavish who was sitting alongside him and the exchange of glances indicated that they both believed that Burken was going on with a load of rubbish.

Burken went on, "The residents committee consequently notified the respondent that it did not consent to the variation of recurrent charges relied on for budget relating to property, insurance and corporate recharge. The balance of the proposed budget was approved and is not in dispute. The residents have responded and engaged in further communications with the operator".

Jones, "One of the things that's been troubling me about this legislation is that since I received the submissions from both sides there doesn't seem to be any protection there to protect a resident - to protect the residents generally from the actions of an operator who was seeking to attribute costs to the residents that were associated with things outside the provision of direct services. I mean, this is the argument that Mr Clarke is putting to us but let's take a ridiculous example. Let's say that the operator - owner operator of the retirement village has a much loved mother-in-law that he wishes to put in as the manager of the village. The normal salary for such a person let's say is $100,000 a year but because of his high regard for his mother-in-law he decides to pay $300,000 a year and that's just charged back to the residents".

"Where is the protection in the legislation for the residents from that sort of activity because you can say that the contract will make provision for the operator to charge back the costs of running the place, the legislation defines the management costs as being one of the legitimate things that can be charged and yet hidden in the budgetary documents we've got a whole list of things and salaries, wages and salaries is included there but there's a dodgy $200,000 included in there that the residents really don't have any opportunity to look into. Now, what's concerning me is that the only way for that issue to be ventilated is for somebody to say salaries look a bit high, I think we should reject the budget and then off it goes to the Tribunal. When it gets to the Tribunal where is my power to look at the reasonableness of the charges? I think that I am very limited in that way".

"That may not have been the intention of the legislation but I think it has to be implicit in the legislation. Unless, Mr Burken, you're familiar with obligation where that is more overt than what I'm talking about. It seems to me that the residents, not just in Pelican Waters but all retirement residents are dependent on the good will of the operator to include only those charges that they're actually charging and legitimately charging. Because there's no way that they can look behind the budget without just rejecting it".

Burken, "You made mention that there's a number of checks and balances for them - being yourself, the CTTT - -".

Jones, "Well - "

Burken, " - -being the budget process, every quarter they receive an actual operating financial statement and to offset discrepancies we report on each line item. The residents don't have to accept that during the budget process nor do they have to accept it during the running of the village. In addition, being a public listed company we take on market prices for staff and we apply that. So - ".

Jones, "So, in this case let's focus down on this case, when the budget was rejected, it's probably an unfair question because I think the position of the residents at that stage was that they're not going to pay any insurance at all and these $28,500 recurrent charges I think that was - well it wasn't open for discussion so, I won't press that line of argument. Mr Burken, have you finished your submissions then?".

Burken, "I believe - - ".

Jones, "I mean I do need to read carefully the written submissions from both sides. At this stage I've only had a fairly brief look at that otherwise anything else you want to add?".

Burken, "I believe the submission covers in detail most of the questions raised by the residents".

Jones, "All right. Mr Clarke, I promised you an opportunity to reply you want to do it now or do you want to have a break for lunch first?

Jack eager to keep the momentum of the case going said, "I'm keen to go on".

Jones, "O.K.".

Clarke "In my reply I'll just sum up - we put our application in stating all our arguments et cetera and received Dollarvill's response and If I can go through certain sections, certain points raised in that response that we feel incorrect or misleading. In Dollarvill's opening statement section 1, point 5, states that during May the balance of the budget was approved. Now that is an incorrect statement, one of the principle objections for the non-payment of recurrent charges on vacant units for which they were responsible. This issue was not resolved until 13 August".

Jones, "Mr Clarke, I don't want to necessarily restrict what you say but in terms of determining the issues today does it matter? I think we need to focus on what's really relevant for making a decision today".

Clarke, "All right, I'll try and stick to the relevant points. The points 14 to 18, and here I refer to the first set of points 14 to 18 not the second points. There's two lots of numbers there, numbered 14 to 18. Here Dollarvill states that none of the items referred to are excluded. The residents contend that two items, two subjects of the application can be excluded in full or in part and these are the issues that separate us. Section 20, points 28 to 30, we contend to prior to receiving Dollarvill's response there was not sufficient detail or transparency in the line items of insurance or corporate recharge to enable the residents to make an informed decision. The detail now provided in Dollarvill's response was previously unavailable to residents despite many requests for more information to be provided".

Jones, "Well, having now got it do you still hold the same position?".

Clarke, "Yes. Section 36 and 48 I'm sorry, point 36 to 48 all refer to the lease of memorandum however, we contend that these are overridden by the Act and regulations and both operator and residents are required to adhere thereto".

"Point 46, we strongly agree with the statement, 20.3 of the agreement for lease confirms that any increase in outgoings will be limited to the residents' share of actual operating costs of the village. I thank Dollarvill for reminding me of that. Point 55, this is a false statement. There was no consultation between the day of the rejection of the budget and 1 June. Correspondence from the residents' committee received no reply".

"In section 5 we have point 62, 63 and 64 regarding insurance and we strongly disagree with these statements. Section 100 of the Act the meaning of four words needs to be considered in determining who is responsible for the cost of the insurance and must, may give an approval. As can be seen from section 100 the village "*must*" be insured by and continue to be insured by the operator. However, the cost of such insurance "*may*" only be met from recurrent charges if approved by the residents as a line item in the budget. For example, Mr Jones, if you knock on my door and say "*May I come in,*" you're seeking permission. If I say, "*Yes, you may come in,*" I am giving permission however, if I say "*you may come in if you wipe your feet*" I'm imposing a condition upon your entry. That is what the Parliamentary draftsmen have done".

"The legislation states insurance may be paid from recurrent charges, however, it places a condition on that and that is, that the action has to be approved by the residents. In the case of this year's budget the residents did not approve the inclusion in the insurance in the budget therefore; we contend that the cost of insurance has to be met by the operator. And our main argument is that we have no insurable interest".

Jones, "I did say earlier Mr Clarke, that I had some obligations in terms of explaining legal issues to you. There are circumstances in which the proper interpretations of "*may*" is that it means "*must*" and that's a matter of interpretation of statute. I will look at that more closely. I take the point your making, it may be that it's conditional, it may be that it means "*must*". It may be that it's optional, I don't know at this stage".

Clarke, "This is typical of the legislation; I know you're not responsible for that. In 71 I even talk about what happened in previous years it wasn't immaterial. Remember that the Act came into force on 1 March this year and operators are now required to conform with the new legislation. We contend that the only significant interest that the resident has in the property is the right to occupy the premises in the terms of the lease. They do not own the property. Despite the fact that numerous requests were made by the committee for detailed explanation of the components that form the recharge this was only provided to residents in general at the budget meeting. We believe that a failure to provide this information to residents as part of a statement of payable expenditure before the budget meeting was a breach of the Act".

"Point 82 of Dollarvill's response, corporate recharge is shown as administration, finance, human resources, information technology. However, in 83 on the next page there was a fifth item, payroll and in the information that was given to the residents at the budget meeting there was a sixth item, property management. The inconsistencies shown here are typical of the way the information is provided to the residents and highlights the difficulties experienced by the residents in obtaining accurate and timely information upon which to make an informed decision. We do not and we don't deny - we don't know or believe if they have been transparent in allocation and apportionment of expenses of Pelican Waters Village and other villages or businesses up until this time. In fact, we believe they have failed to comply with the regulations clause 17.1 (g) the information now available in the response has not been made available to residents and it is our view that lack of compliance means that the issue of corporate recharge was not properly put before the budget meeting and therefore should be removed from the budget".

Jack continued, "Point 96 states, *"The corporate recharge line item cost is similar to previous approved annual budgets for the village"*. We do not disagree with this statement however, the new Act and Regulation requires the operator to be transparent in the presentation of budget. We contend that they were not transparent. In points 98, 99 and 100, these paragraphs make comparison with strata villages where the resident has ownership of a property. At Pelican Waters Village we lease the properties, we are not owners. We do not see the relevance of the argument. In point 115, Dollarvill in making this argument, this is talking about the insurance of the owner, in relation to section 100 (6) this does not include all words from the Act. To properly quote the Act, sub section 6 *"The operator of a retirement village may fund insurance required under this section from the recurrent charges if the cost of any such insurance is included in the approved annual budget."* They left out the word *"approved."* This puts an entirely different complex on it".

"Then we go to the witness statement of Mr Burken, point 132 states that only - -".

Jones questioned, "Whereabouts is this?".

Clarke, "The witness statement of Mr Burken".

Jones, "O.K.. Yes, go on thanks".

Jack continued, "Point 132 states and I quote, *"Dollarvill is a listed company on the Australian stock exchange and as such has to make reporting requirements, a centralised Australian standard has been establish to ensure the efficient processing and the recording of information to meet these requirements and to leverage their economies of scale across Dollarvill's portfolio."* Should we take it to mean that residents of Pelican Waters Village are expected to and indeed do contribute to the cost of these reporting requirements. Reporting requirements have absolutely nothing to do with the

108

operation of Pelican Waters Village. It would appear that Dollarvill is confusing reporting requirements of a listed company with the requirement of recording of finance under the Act. Point 135 would appear, is a reference to 24 hour emergency calls installed in the village. This is paid for by the residents under a separate line item so why is it included here?"

"Point 36, surely all the IT operations listed in 36(a) to (d) are also used by sales staff. I can't find any reference to these costs being split between sales and the village operation. Section 170 of the Act deals with the cost of sales. It shows that the cost of sale are to be shared by the operator and the selling resident. There is no reference to any of the cost associated with sales being paid from the recurrent charge. We know that point 50 states that *"Corporate recharge does not include any sales or related expenditure."* However, nowhere in Dollarvill's documentation is there any detail as to how sales related costs are separated from general operating costs. It is felt that the management of individual residents' contracts are necessarily part of the sales process and as such those costs are Dollarvill's responsibility".

Jack was on a roll and continued, "Point 38 states and I quote, *"It is envisaged that over time reforms implemented by the Federal Government Department of Health and Ageing, retaining all health records of Australian citizens in a centralised data base will be government policy".* Well, what has that got to with the 2010/11 budget for Pelican Waters Village? There is no Federal Government requirement as such and the last I heard the Australian Card was dead. It would appear we're being asked to pay for something that may happen sometime in the future. I would hazard a guess that the present residents of Pelican Waters Village will all be dead and buried before such reporting requirement is necessary".

"Point 40 (a), "*compliance with obligations under the Retirement Village Act (1999) and (2010) Regulations*". I would've thought the compliance of any Act or regulation would be an automatic, compulsory requirement of all public companies and as such the cost of doing business is to be met by that public company and not a cost to be passed onto the elderly residents of a retirement village in which, in our case, over 90 per cent are receiving the Aged Pension".

"Point 40(e) states "*that in part Dollarvill is responsible for the management of residents' meetings*". This is not correct. The residents' committee is responsible for that action the only exception being the yearly management meeting that the owner/operator is now obliged to hold".

"And sub-clause (f), "*Audit fees which are specifically provided to be paid for by the residents under the village contracts*". Point 47 states "*Under section 118 of the Act an operator must ensure the accounts of a village are audited annually.*" Dollarvill does not include audit fees as a separate line item in the accounts; however process of the audit has been discussed with the residents during the budget process. Section 118(2) (a) states that the fees must be itemised in the proposed annual budget. Why is the audit being included in corporate recharge when there is a line item in the budget called auditor with a nil amount. This is just another of Dollarvill's ways of being less than transparent".

"We would suggest that as it is now clear that the residents are paying for the audit on the operational accounts of Pelican Waters Village the next year they will request to have the opportunity to select the auditor. Regarding a statement however, *"The process of the audit has been discussed with the residents during the budget process."* I would like Dollarvill to show where in the documentation evidence that the audit cost was detailed for the residents. As an aside for the information of the Tribunal I would advise the auditor's report for the year ended 30 June 2009 was not accepted by the residents and remains unaccepted to this day. In Amam Lam's witness statement point 23 states that the cost of the audit is $3500".

"Point 41 states that the operator is responsible for the payment of recurrent charges on all vacant units. That is a false statement. Section 159 of the Act gives detail as to *"The requirement of an outgoing resident to continue paying 100 per cent of the current charge for six weeks and thereafter until the property is sold in the same proportion as they are to receive a share of the capital gain unless the contract gives the resident a better outcome."*

"Points 43, 45 and 46 all affirm an exit entitlement calculation. This is a part and parcel of managing an individual residents' contract with the operator and such should not be a cost borne by the residents. 44 is an issue affecting resolution of a matter concerning an individual

111

resident should not involve a cost hidden within corporate recharge. We have a manager who is employed to deal with such matters the cost of whom is met by the residents within the budget".

"I now turn to stand alone insurance quotation, attachment A of Mr Burken's statement. We fail to see the relevance of including a quotation for separate insurance policy for Pelican Waters Village. Residents are not concerned about the cost of the insurance per se. They are concerned that they are expected to cover the cost of the insurance and protect assets in the village wholly owned by Dollarvill. If the findings of this Tribunal are that we do not pay for insurance the quote is not relevant. If the findings of this Tribunal are that we do have to pay for insurance the quote has no relevance".

"The fact is that the village is covered by a policy encompassing all of Dollarvill's villages. Apparently this quote does bring to light a couple of interesting points. Gross profits 1.54 million dollars, cash in transit up to $20,000, payroll including head office, corporate salaries insured for 100 per cent for three years. All these items are in no way related to Pelican Waters Village and are all included in the insurance amount of $23,100. The document is nothing more than a straight out insurance quotation to Dollarvill Limited and there is nothing to suggest that the residents should bear insurance costs in which they have no insurable interest in the property. Any other reputable insurance broker would produce a similar quotation".

"Regarding the loss of profits, Dollarvill makes the profits not the residents. If Dollarvill decides to insure against such a loss the cost should be borne by them, not be borne by the residents. Money in transit and on premises, the only cash involved in the operation of Pelican Waters Village is a small petty cash flow. All the recurrent charges are paid by way direct deposit or cheque. Cash has not been acceptable for the past two or three years".

"Art works and curios, Pelican Waters Villages have none of these. If Dollarvill wish to have artworks in their boardroom at head office why should the residents of Pelican Waters Village be required to pay for the cost of insuring them? There are also references to murder and suicide, are these items included in the present insurance. We don't know. The last shown deducible, or in common terms an excess of $1000 would mean that any claim under that amount will be paid by residents and we suspect is included in the weighted cost of maintenance".

"I point out that up until a week before the directional hearing we didn't know that the excess was $1000 we were told verbally prior to that that it was $5000. Prior to Dollarvill becoming involved in the village the excess was $250. Here it has been attached to the witness statement as an insurance quotation giving a lot of detail. However, residents have not been given any detail as to the present policy covering Pelican Waters Village. There has always been a lack of transparency on Dollarvill's part regarding the insurance policy covering the village".

Jack lifted the glass of water which had been conveniently placed on the table in front of him and took a drink, he continued. "I turn to

Amam Lam's witness statement; the statement by Amam Lam does nothing to convince the residents that we should meet the cost of corporate recharge or insurance. Rachel Stevens witness statement, the manager's witness statement is a generic document with names changed and, one or two line a variation. It matches word for word with another manager's statement produced for another village in relation to a Tribunal hearing. The statement does nothing to convince the residents that we should be meeting the cost of corporate recharge or insurance".

"The information provided by the respondent suggests that management of the village is beyond the capacity of one person and the support provided by head office therefore is absolutely essential. The history of the village does not support that contention because no previous operator has seen the necessity to provide such support and yet there has never been a suggestion the village was mismanaged, rather we believe that generally it was regarded as a successful enterprise and the residents were content. The respondent repeats that being part of Dollarvill team provides opportunities for large savings. That is a statement contradicted by the fact that in our case to join "the team" fees amounting to $28,594 are payable as a share of head office costs. Much is made in these documents of how fair and open management has been in our village. In fact the opposite is true. No replies to correspondence is a regular occurrence. The lack of detail relating to the corporate recharge calculation, the past proposed subsidies in approved budgets by Dollarvill have been reduced without the approval of residents in a contrived end of year figures provided".

"Mr Jones, the residents of Pelican Waters Village again respectfully request you to rule that corporate recharge and insurance be excluded from the budget for the year 2010/11 and in future years and that orders related to such be handed down".

Jones, "Thanks, Mr Clarke, O.K. anything else from you Mr Burken?".

Burken who seemed a little overwhelmed by Jack's reply said hesitatingly, "No I think - - - I don't want to contest a lot of those points which are accurate and inaccurate so I don't think it's worthwhile going down that road - there's a number of inaccuracies and I won't attest to the applicants. I don't think this is the place".

Jones, "All right. That's probably completes the proceedings then but I still have a concern that we may not have fully explored the opportunity to engage in conciliation and I think that with that in mind what I might do if both of you are willing is to have a private conversation with you off the record just the three of us and to see whether there is any way forward that can be found there. If it can't then the hearing is over and I'll go away and think about what you've told me and come up with a decision in due course. So you happy to have a talk Mr Clarke?".

Clarke, "Yes".

Jones, "Mr Burken?" Burken nodded his head in agreement; however without any enthusiasm. "O.K., I'll just turn this thing off for a little while and then we'll - you said there's a room available somewhere close by".

Clarke answered, "Yes room 147 Mr Jones".

The three men went to room 147 and each took a seat around the table. Jones commenced by restating that if he were to make a decision then one of the parties would be unhappy and that it would be much better for all concerned if a compromise could be reached. Jack asked Pierce Burken if he was prepared to offer a compromise, to which Burken replied that the only thing he could offer was the $994 that had previously been rejected by the residents.

Jack then advised that the Committee members present had authorised him to put forward the proposition that if Dollarvill were to reduce the combined amount of insurance and corporate recharge by $15,000 then he was prepared to go back into the Hearing room where the 50 plus residents were waiting and get their approval, Mr Jones could then issue orders along those lines and that would be the end of the matter. This proposal was flatly rejected by Burken.

Jack then requested that he be allowed to return to the Hearing room where he would seek final instructions from those present which he would convey to Mr Jones in a few minutes. As Jack approached the room where his two fellow Budget Committee members and the residents were waiting he could hear the sound of numerous conversations taking place. Jack went to the front of the room and the room fell silent with anticipation.

Jack looked around the room and commenced, "I am sorry but Dollarvill are not prepared to offer anything above the $994 that we have previously rejected. I made a counter offer that we would be prepared to accept a reduction of $15,000 in the combined cost of insurance and corporate recharge, Pierce Burken refused that offer. It is my considered opinion that we have three choices. Number one *"To withdraw our Application"* number two, *"To accept a compromise of a reduction of $994 in Corporate Recharge"* and number three, *"To leave it to the Tribunal Member to bring down a decision, and if it were in the Residents favour to accept the consequences either by the decision being appealed to the District or Supreme Court."* It had been stated by Pierce Burken that Dollarvill would not accept a decision in favour of the Residents and would pursue the matter because of the possible flow on effect to its other villages".

All present unanimously decided to go with the third option and accept the consequences. Jack went back into the corridor where Mr Jones was waiting and conveyed to him the decision of the residents.

Jones then went into the room and after the four Dollarvill representatives had taken their positions at their table he said. "It appears that no compromise can be reached, so I will close this hearing and go away and review all of the information that I have been given and make a decision in three or four weeks when all parties will be advised. Thank you Mr Clarke, thank you Mr Burken".

As the meeting was finished the Dollarvill representatives quickly left the room and the building. Jack turned to Bob and Shirley and said, "Well, I don't know what the outcome will be, but I reckon that we can all go to sleep tonight knowing that we have given it our best shot, we will now just have to wait for the outcome".

Chapter 8

Waiting for the CTTT Decision.

Jack, Bob and Shirley met and reviewed the events of yesterday's CTTT hearing. In view of Pierce Burken's indication that if the residents were successful in their application then Dollarvill would appeal the matter to the NSW District or Supreme Court it was agreed that all residents should be informed of this possibility and that a written report regarding the hearing should be placed in each residents' letterbox as soon as possible. The following report over Jack's name was composed and distributed:

CTTT Hearing:

Pelican Waters Village v Dollarvill Ltd.

Issues: Budget rejected because of the inclusion of Insurance, $23,100 and Corporate Recharge $28,594 (Management Fees)

The Tribunal Hearing which was held at Port Macquarie took 3 hours.

The Senior Member, Mr Jeff Jones reserved his decision, which is expected in writing in 3 or 4 weeks.

I had the 2 other Budget Sub-Committee members at the Table with me although I did all the speaking. There were also some 54 Residents present. Dollarvill was represented by Pierce Burken - Operations Manager, Ron Chaplin from Head office,

Geoff Beard Regional Manager and Rochelle Train Village manager.

Conciliation was the first consideration of the Member; he stated that after a perusal of the Submissions he had not made any decision. He said that if he was to find in favour of the Residents on both counts that this might result in a win for this year's budget but may rebound in next year's budget as the operator might isolate the village from the economies of scale that the operations of a large company give us. e.g.; Insurance this year $23,100 whereas Dollarvill had produced a quotation for the insurance of the village in its own right of $48,000.

Pierce Burken and I retired to a room to discuss a compromise, nothing new was forthcoming, so we were back in the Hearing Room within 5 minutes.

The Member briefly discussed the submissions. I was given the opportunity to make an opening statement, then Pierce Burken replied (not very well I thought) the Member pulled him up on a number of points, particularly in respect to the lack of detail given to Residents with the budget papers. I was then given the opportunity to comment on Dollarvill's submission, which I did by pointing out a number of what we considered to be inaccurate or misleading statements.

Pierce Burken was then given the opportunity to reply but stated that a lot of what I had said was not accurate and which he could refute, but thought that this was not the time or place. My thought was that if this was not the time or place then when will it be appropriate. I am sure I will get an ear full next time Pierce and I meet ☺

Mr Jones then again spoke about conciliation and compromise, and suggested that we again try to reach a settlement only this time with him present and off the record.

During this private meeting the Member again pointed out the danger to the Residents of him making a decision in their favour. I offered a compromise which would have cost Dollarvill $15,000 for the year; this was **not** readily accepted by Pierce Burken.

I then returned to the room with only the Residents present and advised that we had 3 options.

1. To withdraw our Application.

2. To accept a compromise of a reduction of $994 in Corporate Recharge.

3. To leave it to the Member to bring down a decision, and if it were in the Residents favour to accept the consequences either by the decision being appealed to the District or Supreme Court. It had been stated by Pierce Burken that Dollarvill would not accept a decision in favour of the Residents and would pursue

the matter because of the possible flow on effect to its other villages.

The Residents decided to wait for the decision of Mr Jones and accept the consequences. I advised the Member of our decision.

The Member and Dollarvill's representatives then returned to the room and the proceedings were closed.

I am hopeful that at least part of the decision will be in the Residents favour, whatever happens I am sure that Dollarvill or whoever operates Pelican Waters Village at the time of the next budget will be more forthcoming in the amount of detail they give the Residents in the budget papers.

Jack Clarke.

As was customary the following Monday afternoon at four o'clock Jack went to visit his neighbour Frank where a scotch or two would be consumed. Frank told Jack that he had had a phone call from his Share Broker who had advised that Landbuild Limited were making a hostile takeover bid for the shares of Dollarvill Limited. Evidently Landbuild had been in negotiations with Dollarvill for some time, however their advances had not been favourably received and as a result Landbuild were now attempting to acquire a majority shareholding in Dollarvill. The broker had advised Frank that the amount being offered for his shares in Dollarvill was a good price and one that would show him a tidy profit and therefor he recommended that Frank sell.

Frank said that it had been reported in the Financial Review that Landbuild were fast approaching the required percentage to take control of Dollarvill, so Frank like a lot of other shareholders had decided to accept the offer.

It appeared to the two neighbours that it would not be long before Dollarvill would be out of the picture and that the residents of Pelican Waters would be dealing with a much larger company. Both frank and Jack agreed that Landbuild could not be any worse as operators than Dollarvill had been. Neither were sure as to what Landbuild's attitude would be if the Tribunal Member found in favour of the residents.

The following Monday, 22nd November 2010, all residents of Pelican Waters Village received a letter advising them that Landbuild Limited had acquired a controlling interest in Dollarvill Limited and would be incorporating the 30 Dollarvill villages into their existing portfolio of 32 villages in Queensland and Victoria. The letter also advised that there would be a meeting of residents at 11.00am on Tuesday, 30th November in accordance with the Section 41 of the Retirement Village Act, at which representatives of Landbuild would advise the residents of their financial ability to operate the village, and their plans for the future management and operation of the Pelican Waters.

There had been no communication received from the CTTT by the 30th when the meeting of the residents and Landbuild representatives took place.

A goodly number of residents had gathered in the village meeting room in anticipation and perhaps some with apprehension as to what they may learn about this large corporation that had taken control of Pelican Waters Village. At eleven o'clock the Landbuild representatives entered the room. Leading the group was a tall, well-built fellow in his early fifties who introduced himself as Henry Wilson the Australian Manager of Landbuild Retirement Living, which was one of the several divisions of the Landbuild Corporation. Jack was surprised to see that Pierce Burken followed Wilson into the room; also present as expected was Geoff Beard and the village manager Rochelle Train.

Wilson gave a presentation which he had given on a number of occasions within the previous few days and no doubt would continue to give until each of the thirty villages previously operated by Dollarvill had been visited. He gave a brief outline of the size of the Landbuild operation which as well as retirement villages involved shopping centres, industrial complex and residential high-rise developments, and residential housing estates. He stated that at this time there would not be any changes to the existing management structure with Rochelle Train remaining as village manager, Geoff Beard as area manager and Pierce Burken as NSW Operational manager, a distinctive unfavourable murmur went around the room at the announcement about Pierce Burken.

After a short time Henry Wilson asked were there any questions, to which a number of residents responded with questions about their lease contracts and whether there would be any change. The reply was that all contracts remain as is, as it is not possible to alter a contract without the consent of both parties. There were also questions about staffing levels, particularly in respect to the two ground and maintenance employees.

Jack could see that Wilson was anxious to wind the meeting up, so without giving him a chance to do so Jack stood up and waited to be acknowledged. As Jack had positioned himself in a prominent position near the front of the audience he could not be ignored and was duly asked by Wilson for his question.

The room fell silent as Jack commenced, "Mr Wilson, you have doubtlessly been made aware that the Pelican Waters Village Residents Association and Pelican Waters Pty Ltd have been engaged in a matter of dispute in the Consumer Trader and Tenancy Tribunal which resulted from the rejection of the 2010-11 budget".

Wilson said that he was aware of the matter.

Jack continued, "At the Directions Hearing held in connection with this matter the residents advised the Senior Tribunal member, Mr Jones that they were willing to accept the decision of the tribunal and would not contest an unfavourable finding to a higher authority and we requested Pelican Waters Pty Ltd to also enter into such a commitment. Unfortunately, Mr Burken who represented the company refused to enter into such an agreement, also during the Hearing process Mr Burken advised that if the outcome of the Hearing was unfavourable to the company then the matter would be appealed to the District or Supreme Court".

"Mr Wilson I realise that you have inherited the mess we find ourselves in and in an effort to put the matter to rest I now ask you, will you give an undertaking to these residents that if the finding is unfavourable to the company then the umpires decision will be accepted and that will be an end to the matter".

Wilson, who perhaps should have been a Politician, responded that he was not familiar with all the details of the case and therefore could not give such an undertaking at this time. The meeting then broke up with a few residents including Jack, Bob and Shirley going up and introducing themselves to Henry Wilson. Wilson and Burken did not wish to hang around and so with the excuse that they had to attend a meeting at another village left Pelican Waters.

Life in the village went along as usual with the various social events. There was indoor and outdoor bowls, Tai chi and heart moves, aqua aerobics, and Secret Men's Business on Friday afternoons where a group fellows get together with a liquid refreshment or two and discuss a range of things such as current affairs, (so long as it did not involve politics or religion), cricket and football, and experiences that had happened in their earlier days and so on.

Wednesday, 15th December arrived and Jack went to his letter box and took out a letter with the official CTTT logo on it. He hurried home where he sat down in the room he used as his office, opened the letter and read the first page.

The page was headed, *"Consumer, Trader & Tenancy Tribunal"* and on the next line, "Notice Of Order". It went on to give Jack Clarke's name and address together with the case file number and then, *"Application to the Tribunal concerning Pelican Waters Village "*.

Jack was nervous as he read the following; on 9/12/10 the following orders were made:

1. *By consent of the parties the name of the applicant is Pelican Waters Village Residents Association and of the respondent in proceedings is corrected to Pelican waters Village Pty Ltd.*

2, *Pursuant to the provisions of the Retirement Villages Act 1999, s.115(2) (e) an order is made that the line item of "insurance" in the sum of $23,100.00 and the line item of "corporate recharge" in the sum of $28,594.00 are both excluded from the budget for Pelican Waters Retirement Village for the financial year 2010-2011.*

The advice went on to state, *"Enclosed is a copy of the reserved decision from the hearing of this matter on 8 Nov 2010"*. It was signed on behalf of the Registrar and dated 13/12/10.

Jack picked up the phone to call both Bob and Shirley the two Committee members who together with Jack had been instrumental in the composition of the Tribunal Application and Hearing evidence etc.. He phoned Bob first and said, "Bob, I have just received the result of the Tribunal Hearing, at first glance it looks as if we have had a win; however, I would like you to come over and we will go through the "*Decision*" and the "*Reason for the Decision*" together. I will also call Shirley and see if she is available".

Jack thought to himself, "It's too early for a scotch, so I had better put the kettle on for a cup of coffee".

Chapter 9

The CTTT Decision.

Jack, Bob and Shirley sat around Jack's dining room table and went through the CTTT document which detailed the findings of the recent Tribunal Hearing that involved the residents of the Pelican Waters retirement village and the village operator.

The document consisted of fifteen pages, on the first page were detailed the case number, the Applicant, the Respondent, what the application sought, when and where the hearing was held, who represented the two parties and the legislation applicable to the matter.

It was stated that the aapplication was pursuant to Retirement Villages Act 1999, section 115 in respect of approval of annual budget and pursuant to s.108 in respect of approval of a variation in recurrent charges and whether the line item of "insurance" in the annual budget for financial year ended 30 June 2011 should be approved. Also whether the line item of "corporate recharges" in the annual budget for the financial year ended 30 June 2011 should be approved and whether sufficient information is provided by the respondent (the operator of the retirement village) to be satisfied that the requirements of Regulation 26 (e) have been met.

Next listed were the orders given by Senior Tribunal Member, Jeff Jones which stated that the parties had both agreed that the name of the respondent was corrected to Pelican Waters Village Pty Ltd. And pursuant to the provisions of the Retirement Villages Act 1999, section 115 (2)(e) an order is made that the line item of "insurance" in the sum of $23,100.00 and the line item of "corporate recharge" in the sum of $28,594.00 are both excluded from the budget for Pelican Waters Retirement Village for the financial year 2010-2011.

The three sitting around the table looked at each other somewhat in disbelief that they had had such a win. Bob said, "It looks as if the residents will be over $51,000 better off this year". Shirley then reminded Bob and Jack that there was also the $17,000 that the company wanted the residents to pay for the vacant units.

Jack commented, "That's more than $68,000, I wonder just what head office at Landbuild think of that?". Jack continued reading; the next section was "*reasons for application decision*" which were listed under various headings. The first dealt with the applications, one lodged by the operator and the other by the residents. Also listed were the relevant dates of the budget meeting, application dates, directional hearing and hearing dates. It also noted that Mr Jack Clarke represented the residents and Mr Pierce Burken represented the operator.

To avoid confusion, the Residents Association was identified as the applicant and Pelican Waters Village Pty Ltd as respondent. The applications have been heard concurrently and the evidence in one considered as the evidence in both. The document also gave details as to the jurisdiction under which the tribunal operated and that the representatives had made their submissions on affirmation.

The residents submission was listed under nineteen points with reference to seven affidavits and other documents. Then the operators response was listed under ten points with three witness statements. All of which Mr Jones had taken into account.

In his findings the Senior Tribunal Member noted the legislative framework and had copied in five pages of the Retirement Village Act and Regulation.

He then dealt with the insurance issue:

> "The respondent (correctly) points out that the residents are under an obligation to pay the outgoings as that term is defined in the first schedule to the Memorandum of Lease. However, I would caution that any agreement, to the extent that it is inconsistent with the Act or Regulations, is unenforceable".

> "In regard to insurance, the obligation is to pay the lessor's insurance premiums in respect of all buildings, fittings and fixtures against fire, flood, lightning, storm and tempest and in respect of insurance against all other risks referrable to Pelican Waters Village as the Council of Management may deem necessary or desirable".

> "There was no evidence provided in relation to the existence of a Council of Management and whether or not it had deemed any additional risk cover to be necessary or desirable".

"The operator is obliged to have insurance, as per section 100 of the legalisation but the obligation is limited to public liability and damage and costs incidental to reinstatement of buildings".

"The operator is entitled, pursuant to section 100, to fund the cost of such insurance from recurrent charges, if approved in the annual budget".

"In regard to the applicant's argument regarding the use of the word "may" in section 100, I am satisfied that the section effectively gives the operator a discretion by which it may elect either to recover the insurance costs provided for under s.100 as a recurrent charge or it may elect not to do so. If the operator elects to recover the insurance costs as recurrent charges, it can only do so if approved by the residents. It is the refusal of the residents to approve the insurance charges that is now the subject of this application".

"There is no inconsistency between the contractual obligation of the residents to pay insurance costs and the statutory right of the operator to recover costs. The only evidence as to the actual insurance coverage is the quotation provided by the Insurance Broker in the attachments to Mr Burken's witness statement. That quotation specified the insured to be Dollarvill Ltd. and Pelican Waters Village and subsidiary companies. I am satisfied that is entirely appropriate".

"The applicant's argument that the residents have no obligation to pay insurance costs because none of the residents hold an insurable interest cannot be maintained. The property rights are vested in the operator and it is the operator who has an insurable interest and a statutory obligation to take out the insurance. The obligation on the residents to pay for the insurance is not because any or all of them should hold an insurable interest in the property, but because they are obliged to reimburse the operator for the costs it incurs to the extent that they are contractually bound to do so or to the extent that the payments are recoverable by the operator under the provisions of the Retirement Villages Act 1999".

"The quotation from the Insurance Brokers identified the risks as follows; material damage to property insured, consequential loss (business interruption), gross profit, payroll, professional fees, claims preparation. It included cover for infectious or contagious diseases, vermin, pests or defective sanitary arrangements, food or drink poisoning, murder or suicide, works of art, antiques or curios, cash in safe or in transit, replacement of records, loss of land value, etc.".

"Clearly, the insurance cover effected by the respondent goes far beyond the scope of that provided for under s100. Items such as loss of profits, insurance of works of art not located on the premises, cash in transit, etc. are not within the

contemplation of the obligation to insure imposed under section 100".

"The question then is whether there is a contractual obligation under the Memorandum of Lease for the residents to pay additional insurance charges for risks deemed by the Council of Management to be necessary or desirable. There is simply no evidence that the Council of Management has considered the issue. Even if there had been evidence of deeming by the Council of Management, it would still have left the question unanswered as to whether all of the risks insured are "referrable to Pelican Waters Village" as required under schedule 1 of the Memorandum of Lease".

"There is no suggestion that the apportionment formula adopted by the operator in respect of the share of the insurance attributable to Pelican Waters Village is invalid or incorrect. However, I am not satisfied that the whole of the portion of the premium attributed to Pelican Waters Village by the operator is payable by the residents under the Act or pursuant to their individual contracts".

Jones then went on to the corporate recharges issue:

"The fundamental issue for determination is whether or not the amounts charged under the heading of corporate recharge are "costs or fees associated with providing services to residents of the retirement village" (emphasis added). Unless the amounts

included in the corporate recharge come within that exception provided for under Regulation 26(e) the operator is precluded from including the sum in the annual budget pursuant to section 112 and Regulation 26".

"Much of the respondent's submission on this issue related to the methodology for apportionment of the various charges identified. The charges identified that were subsequently apportioned included, administration, finance, human resources, information technology and payroll. It is noted that the headings are somewhat different to those previously advised to the residents as the basis for the charges and considered by Mr McTavish in his affidavit".

"The principle evidence relied upon by the respondent on this issue is the witness statements provided by Mr Burken, Mr Lam and Ms Train. Mr Lam is the financial controller of Dollarvill Ltd. the parent company of the respondent. It would be expected that it would be within his knowledge or capacity to ascertain exactly what the charge is in respect of each heading noted and to identify how that charge is associated with the provision of services to the residents of Pelican Waters Village. That information was not forthcoming in Mr Lam's statement and Mr Lam was not called to give evidence as a witness".

"Mr Burken's witness statement was more helpful on this issue. Mr Burken advised for example that there is a human resources division of Dollarvill Ltd. whose function is to provide the *following services to employees of Dollarvill Ltd: namely personal records and compliance with OHS and other work regulations. There was no explanation of what services, if any, were provided by the human resources division to the residents of Pelican Waters Village".*

"The payroll division was said to provide payroll processing and support for all Dollarvill employees. There was no explanation of what services, if any, were supplied to the residents of Pelican Waters Village by the payroll division. It is noted that the actual cost of the salaries of those employees supplying services to the residents of Pelican Waters Village was not disputed and is dealt with elsewhere in the budget".

"The finance division was said to fulfil the following functions, namely; processing and payment of supply invoices, billing of all residents, preparation and analysis of financial reports including monitoring of the village budget and capital works fund, attending to resident and supply queries, providing support to the village manager with respect to village budget and preparation and issuance of budget notices".

"I think it is self-evident that many of these functions do in fact provide a direct or indirect service to the residents. Some do not. For example, how could the attendance to a query raised by a supplier to Dollarvill Ltd. be interpreted as provision of a service to the residents of Pelican Waters Village? There is some merit in the inclusion of expenses from the finance

division, but there is insufficient information to determine that all the expenses that were apportioned were associated with the provision of services to the residents".

"Likewise, information technology and administration were other areas of activity for which the cost was apportioned partly to the residents of Pelican Waters. The difficulty with all of these charges is that there is insufficient information available for me to draw the conclusion that the whole of the sum that was apportioned to Pelican Waters Village as corporate recharge was in fact for expenses associated with the provision of services to the village".

Jones completed his summary, "With the information available I am unable to say that the respondent was entitled to claim funding of the corporate recharge items from recurrent charges as claimed".

He then went on to detail his decision, "It remains to be considered what the appropriate orders in these two applications are. It is not disputed that the two applications raise the same issues. The applicant does not have a right of action to seek orders pursuant to section 108. It is only the operator that can pursue orders under that provision. Effectively it is the operator's application that orders be made that the two line items in question are approved budget items for the 2010-2011 financial year".

"The applicant seeks orders under section 108 and under section 115. The applicants are not entitled pursuant to section 108 to seek orders under that provision. Section 115(7) provides, however, that because there is an application by the operator under section 108, the Tribunal must first make a determination under any application under section 115".

"I do not believe that anything turns on the issue as the determination, for the reasons expressed above, must be that both the "insurance" and the "corporate recharge" items are excluded from the 2010-2011annual budget".

The document was signed by J Jones, Senior Member, Consumer, Trader and Tenancy Tribunal 9 December 2010.

As Pierce Burken had indicated if the findings of the tribunal went against Dollarvill then they would appeal the matter to the District or Supreme Court. Bob McTavish had researched this matter and found that if an appeal was to be made then the appeal had to be lodged within 28 days of the appellant being notified of the tribunal decision that was to be appealed against.

Jack, Bob and Shirley reckoned that as they had received the CTTT documents on the 15 December they would have to wait until the 12 January to be sure that Landbuild were not going to appeal the matter.

And so the residents of Pelican Waters prepared for Christmas 2010 not sure what the New Year would bring.

Chapter 10

The Appeal Notice.

The 2010 Christmas party was held on Friday 17 December; as usual it was arranged by the village Social Committee with outside caterers providing the meal and various residents contributing to the entertainment. Jack Clarke acted as MC with a string of jokes and a recitation of Banjo Patterson's The Man from Ironbark. He commenced the evening by making an announcement regarding the result of the Tribunal Hearing to much applause from those present; however, he suggested that any declaration of victory should wait till after the 28 days allowed for the company to make an appeal to a higher authority.

Jack then went to a lighter note and told one of his jokes which he always said were true stories, "There was a terrible accident just down the road and three men died. The three got to the pearly gates and were met by Saint Peter. "Look fellows" said Saint Peter said, "*Because there are so many people coming here at this time of year you must each possess something that symbolizes Christmas to get into heaven.*"

The first man fumbled through his pockets and pulled out a lighter. He flicked it on. "*It represents a candle*", he said.

"*That's not quite what I was looking for but o.k., you may pass through the pearly gates and into heaven*" Saint Peter said.

The second man reached into his pocket and pulled out a set of keys. He shook them and said, "*Hear the jingle, Jingle Bells there is nothing more that reminds me of Christmas than Jingle Bells*".

Saint Peter said "*That's not quite what I was looking for but o.k., you may pass through the pearly gates and into heaven* ". He then said to the third man, "*Look, I don't want any more of keys or lighters show me something that symbolises Christmas*".

The third man started searching desperately through his pockets and finally pulled out a pair of women's panties. St. Peter looked at the man with a raised eyebrow and stuttered, "*They... they are ladies panties, how can they symbolize Christmas?*"

The third man replied, "*They're Carols*".

And so the Christmas party went on with everybody enjoying themselves.

On Thursday, 24 December each of the residents of Pelican Waters received a letter dated 23 December on a Dollarvill letter head as follows:

RESPONSE TO TRIBUNAL DECISION

23 December 2010

Dear Resident,

Thank you for your patience during the CTTT Hearing process. As you are aware the Tribunal has handed down a decision in relation to the two line items under review in the current Resident Budget.

Landbuild has just received the information and is currently reviewing it. We will keep you informed once the review has been completed.

Yours sincerely
Pierce Burken
General Manager Operations

On that afternoon, Christmas Eve, Bob McTavish had gone to do some last minute shopping for the long weekend as his two sons and their families were coming for a few days. While Bob was away his wife Beryl, a small frail lady in her eighties who had to use a walking frame to move around and one who was a little timid answered a knock on the door, when she opened it she was confronted by an official looking fellow who announced that he was a Process Server from the Sheriff's Office and that he had a summons for her. Although Beryl had been the wife of a police officer for over 60 years she had never had such an experience like this before and this unexpected confrontation considerably upset her.

When Bob returned he found Beryl upset and on examining the summons found that an appeal had been lodged and that the residents' representative was required to be in the District Court in Sydney on

Tuesday, 8 February 2011. Bob immediately phoned Jack and advised him of the event. From the information contained in the summons it was learnt that Landbuild's legal representative, a Mr Arthur Kedis, presumably with the full knowledge of Landbuild's top management had lodged the appeal documents with the District Court the previous day, the day that Pierce Burken had sent out the letter saying that they were considering the situation.

Jack's response to Bob was, "Well Mate, I have heard of people getting Christmas presents that they didn't want, but this one takes the cake".

As it was the Christmas season the first opportunity that Jack had to inform the residents of this latest development was at the New Year's Day breakfast when a fair number of the residents gathered to partake of a champagne breakfast which started at 8.30am and went through to near mid-day. Jack advised them that the Residents Committee would meet as soon as they were all back after the Christmas break and then call a special meeting of the residents to discuss the matter.

Jack called a Residents Committee meeting for the 11th January. He explained how the summons had been received and the implications of it and what he had done in the meantime to determine how to approach the situation. Jack told the committee that his first call had been to Malcolm McKenzie, president of the Retirement Village Residents Association, (RVRA). Malcolm advised that he would not have been surprised if Dollarvill had appealed the matter to a higher authority; however he was very surprised that Landbuild had followed this course of action considering that they had only recently entered the retirement village industry in New South Wales.

Malcolm was definitely of the opinion that the residents of Pelican Waters were now in need of legal assistance and suggested that TARS (The Aged Care Rights Service) might be of assistance as they had a solicitor who specialised in retirement village matters and did not charge for their services. Unfortunately because of the Christmas break they were not contactable till the previous day and then there was only a secretary answering the phone who suggested that Jack phone back in a couple of days.

Also suggested was Peter Hill of Hill & Co Lawyers at Erina near Gosford on the Central Coast of NSW who was the RVRA's honorary solicitor. Jack was not able to contact Peter as his phone answering service as well as his email indicated that he was away for the Christmas break.

The general feeling of the committee was despondent, they realised the amount of work that Jack, Bob and Shirley had put into preparing for the Tribunal Hearing and now not to have the Umpire's decision accepted by the village operator was most disappointing. There was no idea as to how much it might cost to defend the matter in the District Court or how the residents might fund such an action. It was decided to call a special meeting of residents for the following Tuesday, place the situation before them and be guided by the outcome of that meeting.

On the 12 January each of the residents of Pelican Waters received a type written note in their letter boxes, it was not on a letter head, was not dated and was simply headed, "Notice to Residents", the text was as follows:

> Dear Residents,
>
> In response to the Consumer Trader and Tenancy Tribunal decision for application in which the line items Corporate Recharge and Insurance have been excluded, I wish to advise that Landbuild are still considering all options available and in the meantime have lodged an interim appeal against the decision.
>
> We will endeavour to keep you informed throughout this process and should you wish to discuss this matter further please do not hesitate to contact Pierce Burken or Ron Chaplin.
>
> Yours Sincerely
> Signed, Pierce Burken
> General Manager Operations

At the special residents meeting held on the 18 January 2011, Jack addressed the residents giving a summary of the events to date including the rejection of the budget, the tribunal hearing, the decision of the tribunal. Also mentioned were the letter from Pierce Burken and the summons. Jack also said, "In my opinion the summons which was so rudely delivered to our Secretary's wife by a Process Server states that the Pelican Waters Village Pty Ltd (which is in reality Landbuild) Appeal process is set down for mention in the District Court, Sydney on Tuesday, 8th February. On that date the Judge and Landbuild's legal representative and the Residents representative will confer to set a date and duration for the matter to be dealt with. Other points of procedure may also be determined at that time".

Jack continued, "The advice I am receiving is that we should have legal representation on the 8th February. From what I understand there are at least four possible outcomes. Firstly, the Judge finds in our favour by upholding Mr Jones's decision and awards any costs against Landbuild. Secondly, the Judge finds that Mr Jones was only partially right and varies the Orders so that the two line items are reduced from what they are in the proposed budget. His orders re costs may be for both parties to meet their own costs or otherwise. Thirdly, the Judge finds in favour of Landbuild and over turns the Tribunal Orders and awards costs against us. And fourthly, the Judge finds in our favour by upholding Mr Jones's decision and then Landbuild appeals that decision to the Supreme Court".

"I am of the opinion that Pierce Burken by Appealing this matter to the District Court, by engaging the services of the Arthur Kedis a senior lawyer with Gladsons Lawyers of Sydney and seeking costs against the Residents Association, is basically threatening us with a big stick, with the intention of frightening us off and hoping that we would surrender and now accept the budget that we rejected last May".

Continuing on Jack said, "I am hopeful that Landbuild will back down before the 8th February. I base that hope on my anticipation of the public and potential media involvement, for example last Thursday night the following letter was sent to TV program producers Today

Tonight, Sunrise, A Current Affair, ABC News online, The 7pm Project and Sky News".

HUGE CONGLOMERATE TAKES ON THE "LITTLE PEOPLE"!

Can you imagine anything more perverse than a story about the Landbuild's Group – big business and big profits, taking on a group of elderly pensioners in a Retirement Village to make sure the big business profits get even bigger?

This is such a story!

In the small coastal town on the Mid North Coast where many people go to have a quiet retirement, this story has played out in the past few weeks.

The residents of a Retirement Village felt their operator were not being fair with their costs. So, using the Tribunal which is set up to assist those people with a grievance but who do not have a lot of money for legal fees to fight a case, they went to put their case.

They won! They would not have to pay the $50 odd thousand dollars they felt they were being unfairly asked to pay.

Very happy at having been found correct by the Tribunal they enjoyed Christmas.

Their operator had written to them saying they were reviewing the situation. What the residents didn't know that was rather than reviewing the situation they had already, when that letter was sent employed high legal counsel to drag these "little people" into the courts to defend their money - money which must be a drop in a vast ocean for Landbuild.

There is no end to this story just now – the residents have been told if they want to proceed to the court to fight again for the win they have already had, they should have legal representation. But, where do pensioners get the money to fight a court case against a company with unlimited resources?

Also, in a further intimidator tactic the company is seeking costs from the residents for their legal fees. This makes the whole process a total farce.

Meetings to decide their fate will be held in the coming weeks and this story will have a conclusion.

So, to be continued... ... ...

Jack continues, "The letter was not generated from Pelican Waters Village or anyone connected to a Resident here, and is not attributable to the RVRA. As a result of the above I received a phone call from Norm Lipson of Today Tonight (Chanel 7) whom I spoke to for about 15 minutes and I forwarded to him a historical record of the events. Also as a result of the above letter this issue is being discussed on Twitter and Facebook".

"The RVRA have set up a web site which quotes the letter and gives a history of the events leading up to the receipt of the Summons. This web site was activated at 11.00am last Saturday and to date the page has been accessed numerous times. This gives an indication of the interest and concern that is out there in the community. The Facebook, Twitter, web site and many emails do not necessarily relate to Pelican Waters Village. There are a number of other villages experiencing problems with their operators".

"The media organisations that are showing an interest in this issue are; Today Tonight, Norm Lipson. Choice Magazine, Uta Mihm, Phone interview yesterday, Choice is doing a three page article for the next edition on Retirement Villages in general and she intends to mention the problem that we and other villages are having without naming the village. The Sydney Morning Herald, They have a segment in the pipe line for their finance section to do an article on Retirement Villages, they have suggested that they might now put another item alongside the finance article that highlights some of the problems Residents have with operators. Also Ann Davis, one of the Sydney Morning Herald's investigative journalists has been in contact with a very active Retirement Village friend of mine and is most interested in not only the situation here, but in the retirement village industry generally. That journalist's Mother has just put a deposit on a unit in a retirement village and the Journalist is very interested in what is happening. The Port News, I have been advised that Lisa Tisdale is expected to contact me this week".

The news that the media were interested seemed to lift the spirits of the meeting, Jack continued, "What is it likely to cost? I phoned Peter Hill, the RVRA's honorary solicitor and he advises that the approximate cost for him to appear at the District Court in Sydney on the 8th February, including the time required for revision of the case, possible preparation of submissions etc. would be $1200 to $1500 plus GST. I asked Peter the question, what if the case ran its full course and we lost and the costs were awarded against us what would it be likely to cost. Peter said that with the brief information I had given him, he would not expect the matter to take more than a day to complete. He was also of the opinion that it would be highly unlikely for the District Court to award costs against us because of the nature of the appeal. However, if costs were awarded against us he thought a sum of between $20,000 and $30,000 would be the ball park figure. The District Court has discretion when it comes to awarding costs, so it does not necessarily follow that if we were to lose that we would automatically have to pay costs. Peter also stated that of course if Landbuild lost then he would be asking for our costs to be awarded against Landbuild".

Jack then went on to explain what efforts he had made to obtain pro-bono legal assistance. "I phoned TARS last Tuesday - They advised that they were snowed under, however someone might be able to call me back on Thursday or Friday. A lady named Kim did call on Friday afternoon, unfortunately I was out at the time, I returned the call about 30 minutes later to be advised that she was not at her desk and that she would be requested to call me back. No contact. I also phoned TARS yesterday afternoon to be told that Kim is not in the office on Mondays, I requested that she call me this afternoon. However all the reports I am receiving are that TARS just does not have the staff to cope with all the demands placed on their services".

"I also contacted the Public Interest Advocacy Centre. This is an independent, non-profit law and policy organisation that works for a fair, just and democratic society, empowering citizens, consumers and communities by taking strategic action on public interest issues. Their advice is to try TARS".

As Pelican Waters had about 50% of its residents as member of the RVRA Jack had also spoken to Jan Pritchett the secretary of the RVRA and he advised the residents of the information he had learned from Jan. I have learnt of the *"RVRA Fighting Fund"*, this information is unofficial and I bring it to your attention as I believe that it is relevant to our considerations this morning. The RVRA now has about 5,000 members. The RVRA Committee are in the early stages of establishing a *"Resident Legal Support Fund"* the function of which will be to financially support Village Residents in situations such as we now face. It is expected that the fund will be principally financed from donations from the Membership and or others. Consideration is being given to the RVRA contributing to this fund with a transfer of $10,000 from its accumulated funds. The aim of the fund will be twofold; firstly as I have indicated for the RVRA to financially support its members. Secondly, once the fund is established, operators may think twice about appealing decisions of the CTTT which are favourable to Residents to a higher authority if they know that the threat of the financial burden on Residents is removed by the availability of this fund".

"So where do we go from here. This meeting has to decide what course the Residents want to follow. We are advised that Pierce Burken and Ron Chaplin want to meet with the Residents Committee and the Budget Sub-Committee at 11.00am on Thursday. I consider that it would be inappropriate not to meet with the Landbuild representatives. However what should the committee do at that meeting, I believe we would have to consider three options. 1, It may be suggested that we accept the budget as proposed and rejected last May. 2, We may be offered a compromise reduction of, say 50% off both Insurance and Corporate recharge with the Appeal being withdrawn or, the third option might be that we hold out for the result as handed down and Ordered by the CTTT. That is that Insurance and Corporate Recharge be excluded from the 2010-2011 budget".

"To date there has been no indication of what the proposed meeting with Pierce Burken is about, however your Committee has to be prepared, by having some idea as to what you would like them to do in the eventuality that an offer is put on the table. The biggest problem I have with meeting with Pierce Burken is that I don't know if he is working to his own agenda without the full knowledge and approval of Landbuild Senior Management. I have no confidence in anything that he might say. The past has shown that he is not always as "*fair dinkum*" as I would like".

"Of course we have to be careful in deciding what path the Committee should follow in any negotiations that may be opened up on Thursday. If we were to make a decision at this meeting by way of a formal resolution with a direction to the Committee, I am sure that by Thursday management would hear about it and therefore Pierce Burken would have the advantage of knowing what the Residents had decided".

"If we were to get an indication by way of a show of hands, a majority of those present would have a fair idea of the feeling of those present. I think we should have a "secret indication" as to what you think. This can be done simply by way of a secret written vote. Each will be given a blank piece of paper, simply write on it 1 2 or 3. 1, We give in and accept the budget as proposed last May. 2, The Committee are advised to negotiate on both Insurance and Corporate recharge with the Appeal being withdrawn or 3, we stand firm and hold out for the result as handed down and Ordered by the CTTT".

After a number of questions and discussion from the meeting a secret vote was taken as to what the residents wanted the committee to do. The result which was not disclosed at this time was 97% of those at the meeting were in favour of option three; that was that the committee hold out for the decision as handed down by the CTTT.

There were also motions endorsing the prior appointment of Shirley Dunlop, Bob McTavish and Jack Clarke as being authorised in conjunction with the Members of the Residents Committee to deal with this matter. That if the matter was to be defended in the District

Court, approval of the meeting was given to engage Peter Hill to represent the residents on the 8th February and that his costs for that day be met from Resident Association Funds. Then bearing in mind the rigmarole that Jack had in convincing the Tribunal member that he had the authority to represent the residents a motion was unanimously carried "that Jack Clarke in consultation with the Committee be authorised to instruct and liaise with Solicitor Peter Hill and that Jack Clarke be authorised to attend the District Court on 8th February with out of pocket expenses being met from Association funds".

That afternoon the following email was sent to Peter Hill:

Dear Peter,

Having previously emailed to you copies of the Summons and the Consumer Trader & Tenancy Tribunal Notice of Order. I now advise the following:

> *1.. The Residents of Pelican Waters Village met at 9.30am Tuesday (today) to discuss the issues.*

> *2. The Residents resolved to engage the services of Peter Hill, Solicitor to represent then in the District Court matter on the 8th February 2011.*

> *3. The Residents resolved to meet the costs of any legal representation on the 8th February 2011, from Pelican Waters Village Residents Association funds.*

> *4. The Residents resolved that Jack Clarke in consultation with the Residents Committee and the Budget Sub-Committee be authorised to instruct and liaise with Peter Hill in respect to this matter.*

5.   On Monday (17/01/11) I was advised that the Residents Committee secretary had received a phone call from the village manager advising that Pierce Burken (Operations Manager) and his offsider will be at the village on Thursday at 11.00am and wish to meet with the Residents Committee and Budget Sub-Committee. No further information was supplied as to the nature of the proposed meeting.

6. The residents resolved that a request be made to the village Manager for a copy of the Agenda for Thursday's meeting.

7.   I am posting today to Hill & Company Lawyers at the above address, copies of the submission made to the CTTT by the Applicant (the Pelican Waters Village Residents) and the response by the Respondent Pelican Waters Village Pty Ltd which is a subsidiary company of The Highland Investment Company Pty Ltd a subsidiary company of Dollarvill Limited who were subject to a successful takeover bid by Landbuild about November 2010.

Peter please do not hesitate to contact me for further information.

Regards,
Jack Clarke

The meeting between Pierce Burken, Ron Chaplin, Geoff Beard, Rochelle Train and the committee on the 29th January was held in the meeting room at Pelican Waters village. To say the atmosphere was a little cold would be an understatement. Burken opened by stating that he was regretful of the time and in the manner that the Appeal summons had been delivered; however he stated that the company had no option but to appeal the CTTT decision because of the wide implications that the decision might have in the operation of Landbuilds other villages.

Burken then went on to suggest that it might be in the residents best interests to agree to accept the 2010-11 budget as previously proposed and the company would drop the Appeal.

Jack quickly looked around the table at his fellow committee members and noted that they were all shaking their heads in response to the proposition.

Jack then replied to Burken as follows. "The decision handed down by Jones relates to this village and this village only, it does not set a precedence at law, it applies to the 2010-2011 budget only, Jones has left open the issue of whether Insurance is payable from Recurrent Charges. He made his findings on the fact that you did not give the Residents of this village the detail requested which would have allowed them to make an informed decision about the two line items".

"Landbuild have named the Pelican Waters Village Residents as the Defendant in a matter that we were not responsible for. We did not make the decision that formally excludes Insurance and Corporate Recharge from the 2010-2011 budget, it was the CTTT Senior Member Mr Jones that did that. Why should we have to defend the action of another person or organisation, why didn't Landbuild cite the CTTT or Mr Jones as the Defendant?".

"Landbuild are still in a position where they can get out of this mess and save face, possible even pick up a few brownie points as well. I suggest that Landbuild withdraw the Appeal and accept Jones's decision. They could then make a statement indicating that they had inherited the problem with the takeover of Dollarvill, they had no idea as to the seriousness of the problem and have made this decision as a show of good will not only to the Residents at Pelican Waters Village, but to all Residents within the villages owned and operated by Landbuild".

"The thing that has got the Residents of this village and a lot of other people incensed is the letter received on Christmas Eve which did not give the true facts. The fact is that Landbuild had already lodged the Appeal application the day before we received that letter. And the thing that has really upset everyone is the manner in which we were advised of the Appeal; by way of a Process Server turning up, without forewarning, at the door of our Secretary and delivering a Summons. We consider that to be a very rude way of communicating with the Residents. By citing the Pelican Waters Residents Association as the Defendant, it is each and every Resident in the village that you have cited as the Defendants in this matter".

"I had an email from a lady in Sydney yesterday afternoon who said, *"Maybe we should organise a gaggle of us oldies outside the court on the 8th February, all carrying appropriately worded banners and tell the news coverage that we'll be there? Some of us would do it. I love a street march!!"* I have not as yet responded to the email or its sender" Jack advised

Continuing on Jack said, "Two days ago the residents held a special meeting at which it was resolved by way of a secret vote that we would defend the matter in the District Court and that we would engage legal representation to assist us in this regard".

Burken and his team could see that the residents were not going to give in and that he had a fight on his hands. The meeting closed in the same cold atmosphere as it had commenced.

Chapter 11

The Campaign.

The question of possible costs associated with the District Court Appeal process was a constant worry for Jack and the committee; they knew that there was more than enough in the residents' association funds to cover Peter Hill's costs as estimated for the Directional Hearing. However, if the matter went further, particularly if they lost and costs were awarded against the residents there would be a serious problem.

The RVRA had set up their "*Resident Legal Support Fund*" and were receiving donations from their membership; however, these were limited and Jack did not expect that the RVRA would be able to assist in any great way if the residents lost.

On the RVRA web site they had established a page dealing with the Pelican Waters problem. The first item on the web page was a statement from the RVRA stating their position regarding CTTT decisions being appealed to a higher authority. The statement was as follows:

RVRA position on appeals against CTTT findings.

The RVRA recognises and accepts the right of any party to a legal ruling to appeal that ruling if they believe they have been disadvantaged by errors in law. Specifically, in the case of a Consumer, Trader and Tenancy Tribunal (CTTT) hearing involving the residents and operators of retirement villages in NSW, the RVRA does not seek to remove or deny the right, provided by Section 67 of the CTTT Act, for either the applicant(s) or the respondent(s) to appeal the finding, if they are dissatisfied with the Tribunal's decisions on matters of law.

What the RVRA does contest and seeks to change is the ability and practice of the operator to name the residents as defendants, sole or joint, when the operator chooses to appeal a CTTT finding. The appeal is to challenge the Tribunal's decision on matters of law. These are matters over which the residents exercise neither control nor responsibility, yet if the appeal is upheld they are held responsible not only for their own legal expenses but, most probably, the operator's expenses as well. These can amount to many thousands of dollars.

We believe that this is both unnecessary and unjust. The decision of the appeals court, if it does not affirm the original CTTT finding, can be to either issue its own order overriding the CTTT finding or to order the CTTT to rehear the application, taking into consideration the court's opinions. It is difficult to understand why the residents need to be made party to the appeal for the court to reach these conclusions.

Also, threats by operators, to appeal any CTTT finding favourable to residents, provides the operators with

159

considerable coercive power to deter village residents from exercising the protections provided to them by the Retirement Villages Act. It also nullifies the intent of the CTTT to serve as an accessible, affordable and efficient means of settling disputes.

Malcolm McKenzie, President
Jan Pritchett, Secretary
24th January 2011

The second web page item was the article *"huge conglomerate takes on the "little people"!* Which Jack had quoted to the residents at the special meeting held on 18th January.

The third item was a four page summary of events relating to the matter and written by Jack Clarke.

Then there were twelve letters from various retirement village residents from around the State, all expressing their concerns about the Pelican Waters situation. A sample of the letters is as follows:

It is indeed galling to see a large corporation contesting a CTTT finding of $51K, a pittance to them, made in favour of a group of retirement village residents. But I suppose it is naive to expect them to act other than in their own self-interest. The increasing corporatisation of Retirement Villages bodes ill for their residents.

When I first read your report of the CTTT ruling some weeks back, my initial reaction was that, while you and your village had a pleasing win for this year, next year Landbuild would undoubtedly be back with more detailed documentation and justification to support their proposed budget. I gather that this was your expectation also.

But I also expected that, given the potential costs of appealing, Landbuild would write-off the $51k to experience and not appeal the finding. Wrong again! That is thinking like a retiree with shallow pockets, not a corporate executive with deep pockets and a cadre of lawyers available. From your latest report, it seems that from the beginning they were planning to appeal if they lost. Presumably they saw it as a landmark case, not only for their own villages but the whole NSW industry.

From my understanding of Section 67 of the CTTT Act, I'm curious as to what are matter(s) of law on which they will base their appeal. From your latest report, I'm having difficulty in identifying what "matters of law" in the finding that Landbuild's lawyers can find to object to.

On the insurance matters the Member

- *Upheld their right to include the (allowable) premiums in recurrent charges*
- *Drew their attention to the limitations outlined in Section 100 of the RV Act*

As regards the Corporate Recharge (cost allocations) he;

- *Pointed out that there needed to be a direct or indirect benefit to the residents.*

- *Did not rule any particular item in or out, merely commented that the inadequate documentation provided both in the budget and at the hearing, failed to identify the benefits to residents.*

What is/are the matter(s) of law arising from those findings? Or do I need to be a corporate lawyer to be able to identify or manufacture sufficient grounds for an appeal? I suspect the answer is "yes".

To me, the iniquitous part of the whole process is not that the losers in a CTTT finding have a right of appeal.

The right to appeal an unfavourable verdict is an integral and necessary part of our legal system in all jurisdictions. Rather it is the consequences of a successful appeal. If the appellant is successful, the defendants have to pay not only their own considerable legal fees but, most probably, also those of the appellant, even though no fault attaches to them. Any errors in law found by the appeals court were made by the CTTT member(s) who conducted the hearing, not the defendants.

It is also that the mere threat by a village operator to appeal a CTTT finding, thus involving a group of retirees in open-ended legal expenses of unknown magnitude, can be such a deterrent as to nullify the whole concept of the CTTT as an affordable, accessible and efficient means of resolving disputes.

It is truly a case of punishing the innocent and is a matter that needs to be addressed. In a case such as this I do not see why the CTTT should not be the one and only defendant.

Regards

Another letter on the RVRA web site was:

There has to be a better way to live together!

The Pelican Waters Residents Committee didn't make the rulings that Landbuild have now appealed to the NSW District Court. The rulings were official decisions made by CTTT stating that certain expenses are not to be allowed to be included in their residents' annual budget.

Surely, if Landbuild wished to appeal the CTTT ruling, then Landbuild should have gone back to a CTTT "higher authority" for their challenge, but not take the Residents Committee to another court.

Additionally Landbuilds want the District Court to rule that their substantial costs of employing lawyers to conduct the case should be paid by residents if Landbuilds won the appeal!

Seemingly from this case, the problem starts with managers deliberately intending to deprive residents financially by adding unsubstantiated expenses into budgets. That itself is wrong as morally managers have a duty to protect residents' interests before owner's finances.

By Landbuilds' declaration to fight the decisions made against them they have indicated their disrespect of residents' rights. Such conduct opposes the way of life adopted by the majority of the perceptive elderly in their villages who have been raised with honourable principles but who are nevertheless financially vulnerable.

If this sort of thing is allowed to continue there will certainly be a run of residents leaving villages. Once they leave these same people will no doubt spread the word to friends and family about the futility of living in any village operated by owners using unfair methods.

Most villagers enjoy community life but are now hearing more and more how poorly certain villages are being run by managers and owners, who seem to be displaying an appalling lack of understanding of the rights and financial status of the majority of the elderly (many of whom are pensioners). Some of these owners appear to be ignoring new legislation too.

Owners of villages linked to the Retirement Villages Association, who will apparently represent them legally, should know that there is a growing number of residents who are now well aware that they have been, and are still being, unfairly treated financially by some operators.

Operators should recognize that there are still a lot of old 'fighters' who were raised through depression years who will continue to use their fighting spirit. Being locked into their last "Valhalla" they will no doubt spend their remaining days challenging on-going unfair practices.

Is there a solution to balance all this up? Yes, if both sides are willing to sit down together, adjudicated by an independent legal body, to draw up fair, reasonable rules involving transparent acceptance of specific expenses. When a plan involving acceptance of responsibilities is finally decided, both parties then request relevant Government legislation.

Until that happens the whole industry will continue to deteriorate meaning all stakeholders will lose out.

Owners will probably lose a whole lot more than both residents and Government because owners will find it harder and harder to get new tenants to live in their villages when the word gets out to the public, including residents' adult children who may plan to enter a village and who are increasingly confused and becoming anxious about the present situation.

The reference to the RVA in the above referred to the "*Retirement Village Association*", this was an organisation representing retirement village operators.

One resident of a retirement village took the trouble to write to all NSW Politicians as follows:

Dear NSW Parliamentarians

"Government of the people, by the people, for the people" has a nice ring to it, does it not? If only it reflected reality. All too often government turns out to be not for the people, but rather for the big end of town and others whose vested interests run counter to the common weal.

Such is the case with the retirement village industry, obviously seen by the aforesaid big end of town as a growth industry and avenue for profitable investment. So they are buying up single and groups of villages and bringing them into the corporate fold. It is reminiscent of what happened to the childcare industry some years ago. Does ABC Learning ring a bell?

So the residents of those villages no longer find themselves dealing with an owner/manager with a personal involvement in the village and with the residents whose lives they share.

Now the villages are managed by hired staff, whose actions and attitudes are dictated by a corporate headquarters that appear to see their residents primarily as an irritating, vexatious but necessary source of funds, from whom the maximum amount possible is to be extracted.

In such a climate, disputes between residents and operators arise. For residents, their primary protection is the Retirement Villages Act, which promotes the usage of the Consumer, Trader and Tenancy Tribunal (CTTT) as a means of resolving disputes in an informal, expeditious and inexpensive manner. Legal representation is discouraged in normal circumstances.

*It achieves these objectives if, and only if, both sides accept the CTTT finding. But the CTTT Act also allows an appeal to the District Court if either party is dissatisfied with the finding **on a matter of law**. That's when things get serious as regards legal representation and expense. A solicitor, at least, is recommended; quite often barristers are also briefed.*

When their opponents are either pensioners or self-funded retirees, obviously it gives a significant advantage to a large corporation with deep pockets and a cadre of specialist lawyers, available through their industrial organisation, the Retirement Village Association.

This advantage can and is used, not always subtly, to suggest that if the residents take an issue to the CTTT, and succeed; it will be appealed, thus potentially exposing the residents to legal expenses of uncertain but considerable magnitude. If the residents refuse to be intimidated and successfully proceed, then the same threat can be put into action. For the details of such a current situation here in NSW the RVRA web site.

Under the CTTT Act the operator can only appeal on matters of law. That is they are claiming that the CTTT members got it wrong in law when making their findings. But it is the residents who invariably are named as defendants. If the appeal succeeds, it is they who have to pay not only their own legal fees but, most probably, also those of the operator. This can run into many thousands of dollars. I find it iniquitous that the residents must pay for any legal errors made by the CTTT member(s) conducting the hearing.

The only alternative available for the residents is not to defend the action. In this case, the judge may well make an order for costs against them. Is that just?

To my lay mind the solution to the problem is clear. When leave to appeal against a CTTT finding is granted, as it is based on matters of law for which the residents have no responsibility, they should be excluded as defendants. But that will require legislative action, which is why I am addressing this to you, in the hope that remedial action will follow.

Sincerely

In response to the above a number of NSW Politicians sent letters to the NSW Minister of Fair Trading, the following is from an Independent Member of the Legislative Assembly.

Dear Minister

Retirement Village CTTT Appeals

I write on behalf of constituents concerned about risk for retirement village residents when a Consumer Trader and Tenancy Tribunal (CTTT) decision is appealed.

A number of residents have raised concerns that an application for appeal by Landbuilds against a CTTT decision in favour of Pelican Waters Village Residents Association will put residents at risk of significant legal fees, and potential costs if the District Court awards costs against the Association, who made the initial application to the CTTT.

Residents say that the growth in for-profit retirement villages will result in more appeals against decisions that favour residents, and retirement village owners will use their much greater resources to discourage residents lodging claims with the CTTT.

Those who have contacted me are concerned that the Retirement Villages Act aims to provide quick and accessible low cost avenues to address disputes.

Could you please consider this case and the concerns raised, and inform me what action you will take?

Yours sincerely.

Another from an Independent Member of the Legislative Assembly.

Dear Minister,

I write on behalf of many constituents of my electorate, and in particular the residents of Pelican Waters Retirement Village, regarding concerns over the upcoming appeal against a Consumer Trader and Tenancy Tribunal decision.

Whilst it is important that there is no denial of natural justice to parties wishing to appeal legal decisions, it is also important to emphasise the significance of this case in setting precedents for other Residents' Associations who may wish to use provisions of the Retirement Villages Act to have a dispute settled by the CTTT at reasonable cost.

Given the significance of this matter to all residents of for-profit retirement villages in NSW, it is important that this test case Is resolved fairly, with equal access to legal representation, and with confidence that residents will not face undue financial burdens as a consequence of meeting the appellants in higher courts. It would be a great disappointment if the provisions of the Act which were designed to provide a measure of engagement and financial scrutiny for residents, were rendered hollow by the respondent's inability to underwrite a robust legal examination of the facts.

I would welcome your consideration of these concerns, and look forward to your early advice.

The Shadow Minister for Fair Trading wrote as follows:

Dear Minister

Retirement Village Appeals from the CTTT

It can be disturbing and unsettling for residents when village management appeals a decision made by the Consumer, Trader and Tenancy Tribunal. Legal costs are also a real concern.

Numbers of residents of retirement villages are writing to me with particular concern about the actions of Landbuild Retirement Living in appealing a decision of the CTTT as to the degree of information to be provided by operators to residents in presenting annual budgets for approval.

It is of genuine concern that, having won their case before the Tribunal, a selection of volunteers from among the residents of Pelican Waters Village are now facing the effort, stress and expense of an appeal and the threat of adverse costs orders.

Here is a matter where the industry and consumers need clarification of a key part of the budget process. Traditionally it is through the appeals process that true precedent can be set - see sections 65 and 67 of the Consumer, Trader and Tenancy Tribunal Act 2009.

The Tribunal is inadequate for this task. However, given the specifics of this case, I ask that you review what action you can take to bring the parties into mediation and to develop guidelines on budgetary disclosure. We can all expect further applications to the CTTT and appeals to the courts as the new budgetary process settles down and the new legislation tested. Improved guidelines, in the context of industry and consumer consultation, are needed.

It might be appropriate to investigate funding for the present appeal itself as the decision will be of significant wider precedent value.

In view of the importance of these issues, and the anxiety being suffered by so many village residents across the state as they watch the unfolding of this crisis, I ask that you take action with all due urgency.

Yours sincerely

There were in total some 77 letters sent to the RVRA which were placed on their web site, typical of these were:

Sent by email to the RVRA Secretary, 31/11/10

Hi Jan.

A mild rant on my part and a commitment to attend the court hearing on the 8th Feb.

In my mind the concept of retirement villages is not the preserve of Landbuilds or any other village owner. The concept did not originate with them nor should they enjoy the freedom to dictate their wants at the expense of a significant segment of the community. Landbuilds or another company owning all or most of the retirement villages in the country is an ugly thought; I make the assumption that Landbuilds performance would be similar to the operators of the village I reside in.

At its very basic a retirement village is and should be a partnership between those prepared to build and operate, those who choose to live in such villages and the forces of law and order who establish rule and regulation to make the retirement village environment suitable to meet the needs and wants of both parties. Equity and fairness, justice and the recognition of the true needs of the elderly should be reflected in the rules and regulations and I do not think they are. If they are not then all endeavour should be made to ensure change to effect the needs. And I guess that is happening slowly and painfully.

There are many interested parties involved in the affairs of retirement villages but one party seems to lack an appropriate place in the debate and that is those living in the villages. This is so to the extent of distinct bias on the part of government and industry, leaving only the RVRA to carry and project the high level of dissatisfaction experienced by village residents.

Representation on any and all organisations which have an interest in the industry seems to me to be the only way that the voice of those most affected will ever be heard.

Raising the profile and voice of village residents via laws which place representatives in positions to effect some participation in and contribution to the standards of the industry may bring a more practical and realistic relationship between owners and residents.

Some of the letters were quite long; others such as the following one were short:

I would like you to know that several of my friends at my village are incensed at what is happening re the CTT Tribunal relating to the Pelican Waters residents.

Landbuild are acting as a bully no less to those residents I am sure if more people in NSW were aware of their actions there would be an uproar.. Sadly there are so many other issues that hit the headlines but I would like you to know that we fully support the RVRA in drawing attention to politicians about the dreadful behaviour of Landbuild.

The support that the Pelican Waters residents received by way of letters to the RVRA was most encouraging, another read as follows:

The Pelican Waters Village saga clearly illustrates just how the almighty dollar and greed has clouded the spirit and reasonable expectations of two willing parties executing a retirement village contract, and how this has ended up in court.

Taking this case at face value, one must wonder how such a document agreed to, signed and sealed by both parties could ever reach the stage demonstrated in the correspondence.

Does this mean that the document is flawed, or so complex that the owners Legal experts can troll the document to escape their obligation or win the argument?

If this is yet another case of "My pocket is deeper than yours" strategy applied by some corporate bullies, then mere mortals like retirement village residents have little hope of winning unless they either engage expensive lawyers or simply appeal in court alone.

The problem is that this style of bullying tends to win out by simply wearing out their opposition by some sort of moral protection for the wellbeing of their shareholders etc.

Then there is the case, dare I say it, where the owner becomes the victim with lessees playing that game in reverse.

Unfortunately we now live in a society where a shake on the hand is well gone and sorting out many pages of clauses drafted by lawyers for lawyers to escape moral and technical obligations prevailing today.

When that happens the system breaks down and all that is left is no winners and empty pockets.

I feel very much for Pelican Waters Residents and trust that the powers that be responsible for justice in this area will get their head out of the sand and exercise their trusted position by seeking justice for all parties.

There were many other and similar letters being posted on the RVRA web site. Jack realised that all of this interest the RVRA web site was creating was good; however he was concerned that the high-ranking management at Landbuild may not be aware of the situation. Jack penned the following letter which he sent to the Chairman of the Landbuild Board and a copy to each Director.

Dear Sir,

Re: Pelican Waters Village, Laurieton.

I write to you as a Resident of the above village which is now owned and operated by Landbuild Retirement Living.

In short the problem is that in May 2010 the Residents of the village rejected the budget as proposed by the then operator Dollarvill Limited. The reason for rejection was a lack of detail in respect to two budget line items, which is contrary to the retirement Village Act 1999. As a consequence the matter was

176

taken to the Consumer Trader and Tenancy Tribunal (CTTT) and in due course on the 9th December 2010 the CTTT handed down Orders that the Line Items of "Insurance" and "Corporate Recharge" were to be excluded from the 2010-2011 Budget. This order relates only to Pelican Waters Village and for this year's budget only.

On the 23rd December 2010, Landbuild Retirement Living lodged an Appeal with the District Court with the Defendant being named as the Pelican Waters Village Residents Association. I acknowledge that operators of retirement villages or the Residents in retirement villages have the right to appeal a decision made by the CTTT. However, I am opposed to the naming of the Residents as the defendants, which is unnecessary, unjust and gives the operators considerable coercive powers to deter the residents from exercising their legal rights. For after all it was not the Residents who handed down the decision, but the CTTT.

To examine more detail in respect to this matter may I suggest that you have a look at the Retirement Village Residents Association (RVRA) web site, particularly I respectfully ask you to look at the first three links (1, 2 and 3) on that page. There are many other links to various letters etc. that have been received from Residents in other villages as well as Politicians.

Last Thursday, the Pelican Waters Residents Committee and Budget Sub-Committee met with Management Representatives; Pierce Burken, Ron Chaplin, Geoff Beard and Rochelle Train. At that meeting I put forward the proposal that if Landbuild were to accept the CTTT decision and remove the two line items from the budget for this year and withdraw the Appeal Application which is set down for mention on the 8th February, then the Committee and Residents would approach the forthcoming budget with a clear and open mind considering the assurances from Management that sufficient detail will be supplied for the Residents to make an informed decision.

I also advanced the suggestion that Landbuild could still come out of this without egg on their face and possibly pick up a few brownie points, not only with the Residents at Pelican Waters but also with retirement village Residents throughout Australia. This could be achieved by accepting the above proposal and making a statement that Landbuild had inherited this situation with the takeover of the Dollarvill Group and now having investigated the position they were willing to abide by the CTTT decision.

My proposal was given only a lukewarm reception with the comment that it would be discussed in Sydney. Nothing has been heard to date.

Sir, your assistance in sorting this mess out before it gets into the District Court will be greatly appreciated.

Yours faithfully,
Jack Clarke
27 January 2011

As well as letters being posted on the RVRA web site Jack had sent out an appeal to numerous people who he thought might be interested in the matter requesting them to use Face Book and Twitter to further put pressure on senior Landbuild management. One particular approach was to send an enquiry through Landbuild's Retirement Living web site asking something like this, *"Was it common practice for the management of Landbuild retirement villages to treat all of their residents in the same dictatorial and stand over manner that the residents of Pelican Waters village were at present being subject to as detailed in the matter before the NSW District Court"*.

Another typical email sent to the Manager of Landbuild Retirement Living was, *"My Grandmother is in a retirement village operated by Landbuild, is the situation as described on the RVRA web site typical of how you treat all your village residents?"*

Each enquiry received a similar answer along the lines of, *"This dispute has arisen because of a lack of clarity in the NSW retirement village legalisation, by appealing the matter to the District Court it is hoped that a clearer definition between what the village operator and the resident is responsible for will be determined"*.

At the regular residents meeting held on Tuesday, 1 February Jack reported to the meeting as follows; "Yesterday afternoon I had a 30 minute phone consrersation with Peter Hill, he asked a number of questions about items relating to the Budget and CTTT case. Landbuild have Appealed the CTTT decision on the grounds that the decision was illegal. Both Peter Hill and I cannot understand what

179

logic they are applying to reach that decision. Peter does not know what will happen next Tuesday at the District Court. As the matter is set down for mention there are at least four things that could happen. Firstly, the Judge will decide upon a date and length of time for a Hearing at some time in the future. Secondly, the Judge may decide that this is a simple matter and deal with it there and then. Thirdly, the Judge may decide that the Appeal should not go ahead in the District Court and refer the matter back to the CTTT and fourthly, the Judge may disallow the Appeal and throw the matter out. We will not know till next Tuesday".

On the 2 February, Bob McTavish and Jack received a letter from Henry Wilson, CEO of Landbuild Retirement Living, as follows:

Dear Mr Clarke,

Thank you for your letter dated 27 January to Landbuild's Board of Directors regarding Landbuild's decision to appeal the Consumer Trader and Tenancy Tribunal (CTTT) decision in regards to Pelican Waters Retirement Village; I'd like to assure you we are taking your correspondence very seriously.

I appreciate that this matter is causing considerable concern for residents and I would like to explain Landbuild's position.

We take on board the comments by the CTTT that we should have provided a higher level of transparency during the budget process. This level of detail was most definitely provided at the CTTT and we are reviewing our systems to ensure an appropriate level of disclosure is provided in future budgets.

Landbuild does not think that the CTTT decision in removing the whole line items was appropriate or consistent with how the resident contracts and the Act work. As we understand it, Landbuild and the residents of Pelican Waters agree that there should be some charge for insurance and corporate recharge in the budget in accordance with resident contracts and the Act.

Rather than determining what this amount should be, in this case the CTTT removed the items altogether. This outcome does not provide clarity for residents or operators about how these charges should be handled in the future.

To resolve this matter In the fairest possible way Landbuild proposes to pay the legal costs for the Residents of Pelican Waters Retirement Village up to $50,000 with legal representation of the residents' choice completely independent of Landbuild.

The residents of Pelican Waters will have full authority and responsibility for engaging and directing their own legal counsel. In addition, Landbuild will pay our own legal costs in seeking clarification on this matter. This will ensure we all receive legal clarification for this matter at no personal cost to residents. Similarly, Landbuild would agree not to pursue any costs orders that may be made by the District Court in its favour.

We also suggest an adjournment of the District Court hearing to a date later than the currently scheduled date of 8 February. This will allow more time for you to prepare.

Our lawyers will formalise this proposal and contact Mr Jack Clarke, President of the Pelican Waters Residents Committee with the appropriate documents.

We do regret that this matter has become a source of confusion and anguish and that it has taken a long time to address.

Sincerely
Henry Wilson
CEO – Landbuild Retirement Living

This was indeed a turn around and an unexpected response to Jack's letter to the Chairman of the Board. The letter was discussed with the committee and with Peter Hill. Correspondence was also received from Ms Smith of Gladsons Lawyers advising that they were acting on behalf of Landbuild Retirement Living and confirming the proposed arrangement re costs.

The following day Peter Hill responded to Gladsons as follows:

Dear Ms Smith,

We act for Pelican Waters Village Residents Association in relation to the above appeal.

We are in receipt of your letter to our client of today's date and have had an opportunity to now take instructions.

We attach a copy of the Notice of Appearance and Notice of Contentions that was forwarded to the District Court Registry today for filing and will provide a sealed copy once returned from the Court.

Our client accepts your clients offer to meet our client's legal fees as well as both sides agreeing not to pursue costs against the other if successful as outlined in your letter.

Our client does not agree with an adjournment when the matter comes before the Court next week and believes that this matter needs to be dealt with expeditiously. Our client is ready to run the matter as soon as possible. We understand that the matter will be a Directions Hearing next week. We anticipate that the hearing will run for approximately half a day and given the nature of the matter, the leave for appeal question be dealt with at the same time as the substantive appeal (obviously though subject to the Court) . It is not a complex matter.

To this end we propose that the Directions require the Plaintiff prepare an appeal book (with transcript) and provide to defendant for review and agreement within 7 days and within

10 days, this be filed with the Court. Following this, we seek the earliest possible date for hearing.

We look forward to hearing from you as soon as possible and agreeing on appropriate Directions for the speedy hearing of this matter.

Kind regards,
Peter Hill

Evidently the above was agreed to as there was no further suggestion of an adjournment.

Chapter 12

The District Court Directional Hearing

Tuesday, 8 February arrived. Jack was out of bed at 4.45am to enable him to get to the Port Macquarie airport by 6.00am in order to catch the first flight of the day to Sydney which left at 6.30am. The flight was on time arriving at Mascot at 7.40am. After travelling to Central by train Jack had time for a good breakfast at a small café in Eddie Avenue before walking up to Goulburn Street.

Jack took a copy of the Court Appearance notice from his coat pocket to check the address he was heading to, John Maddison Tower, 86 Goulburn Street, Sydney. The time set down for the Directional Hearing was 9.30am. At 8.55am Jack arrived at the lobby of John Maddison Tower, an impressive building of 27 floors. Jack proceeded to the security checking area; he emptied his pockets and placed the contents into a tray which went through the x-ray machine. As the previous year Jack had been fitted with a pace maker he did not go through the security metal detector but went to the gate alongside it and beckoned to one of the three security officers on duty. He explained that he had a pace maker and the officer let him through the gate to an area off to one side where he proceeded to give Jack a 'pat down' to make sure that he was not carrying any offensive weapons or other prohibited items. All being well Jack retrieved his belongings from the tray which had passed through the x-ray machine and preceded to the lift area where on the walls were listed the hundreds of cases that were to be dealt with that day. He quickly found the listing for the Pelican Waters matter and took one of the several lifts to the 7th floor.

On exiting the lift Jack observed that there were a number of Court Rooms located on the 7th floor, finding the one he was looking for he had a look inside and found that there was nobody there. Jack's mobile phone rang; it was Peter Hill advising that he had been held up in traffic; however he believed that he would arrive in time. After a couple of minutes of being what appeared to be the only person present people started to arrive from the lifts, among the first were Malcolm McKenzie and Jan Pritchett, the President and Secretary of the RVRA whom Jack was pleased to see as this indicated that the RVRA had its full support behind the residents of Pelican Waters he was not on his own in this fight with one of Australia's biggest companies.

It was not long before the corridor had a large number of people in it, including a goodly number of retirement village residents who had come along to give and show support for the Pelican Waters residents. The residents upon realizing that it was not a large Court room went in and took a seat and in no time at all every seat was occupied by elderly village residents.

All of the legal people who were there then had to stand in the centre isle of the court room in order of the listings for the various cases. Peter had requested Jack to find the Solicitor representing Landbuild and to advise him/her of his situation. Jack soon located the Solicitor from Gladsons Lawyers, Ms Smith and advised her that Peter expected to be present shortly. Ms Smith and an offsider, evidently a junior solicitor, indicated that that would be o.k. and if Peter did not turn up on time she would request that the matter be held over till the end of the Direction Hearings.

At 9.30 am a District Court Registrar's Associate entered the Court room from a door behind the bench with a bunch of folders under her arm, after the young lady had put the folders in order and taken her seat a Court Officer entered from the same door and announced, "All Stand' and the Registrar entered and bowed to those assembled, the legal persons present acknowledged the Registrar also with a bow with the residents following suit, the Registrar, Mr C. Brown took his seat. Those that had seats, who were only the residents, were then seated; however there were about thirty Solicitors and their assistants lined up, presumably in the order that they were listed for the morning's proceedings.

Shortly after Jack's conversation with Ms Smith, Peter Hill arrived and after greeting Jack, Malcolm McKenzie and Jan Pritchett, Peter spoke to Ms Smith. Peter Hill and Ms Smith then took their place towards the back of the line of solicitors who were all waiting for their cases to be called. A variety of matters were dealt with by the Registrar, each case was identified by a file number and the names of the Applicant and the Respondent, the proceedings all revolved around the setting of dates and times for the hearing of the various matters.

After about fifteen minutes the Pelican Waters matter was called, Ms Smith introduced herself as representing the Applicant, Pelican Waters Pty Ltd and Peter stated that his name was Peter Hill and he was a registered solicitor and the Practice Manager for Hill and Company Lawyers and that he was representing the Pelican Waters Residents Association.

The Registrar asked, "How many days will be required to finalize the matter?"

Ms Smith jumped in and said, "We believe that the matter will take at least three days Registrar".

The Registrar looked at Peter Hill and asked, "In your opinion Mr Hill, how long will be required?"

"This is not a complicated matter Registrar, one day should be sufficient for the Court to reach a decision" Hill replied.

Ms Smith came back with, "Registrar, this case could have far reaching effects on the retirement village industry in this State, perhaps if two days were allowed for at this time, further hearing days could be arranged if the presiding Judge thought it was necessary".

There then ensued discussion as to suitable dates and it was agreed that Monday, 14th and Tuesday, 15th March were acceptable dates to both parties.

Smith and Hill then left the Court room and had a brief discussion in the corridor after which Ms Smith and her assistant left. The retirement village residents who had travelled into the city from various outlying areas as well as from the Central Coast, had also left the Court room and were all standing around talking amongst themselves. Jack went to Peter Hill and suggested that it might be appropriate to thank the residents for turning up and requesting their support at the Hearing on the 14th and 15th March, to which Peter readily agreed.

The thirty plus residents were gathered into a group and addressed by Peter Hill, he explained to them just what this morning procedure was, briefly what would happen at the Hearing next month and suggested that the residents of Pelican Waters had a strong case; however the support of a group similar to today would be greatly appreciated at the Hearing and he thanked them all for their interest in the case.

Jack and Peter agreed that they would confer by phone the next day to discuss if any further documentation would be required. Jack was also assured that the $50,000 plus GST would be sufficient to cover Hill and Company Lawyers costs in the matter.

As it was now only 11.00am and Jack had hours before he had to be at Mascot to catch his flight home, he and Malcolm McKenzie, Jan Pritchett, together with two RVRA Committee members and a couple of other active residents decided to have an extended lunch and discuss various matters of concern to the retirement village residents. The group walked down to the Masonic Club in Castlereagh Street where as well as lunch a fruitful couple of hours were spent in discussing matters relating to retirement villages.

Jack was at Mascot in time to change his flight from 5.20 to 4.10pm which got him back to Port Macquarie at 5.20pm and then home by 6.00pm. While waiting at Mascot Jack phoned Bob McTavish to let him know what had transpired that day and asked Bob to convey the same to Shirley Dunlop.

The next day Jack composed and sent out the following report to each Pelican Waters resident:

To the Residents of Pelican Waters Village.

Dear Fellow Residents,
As your elected representative in respect to the ongoing Tribunal matter I submit the following for your information.

Report of District Court Directional Hearing:
The (Landbuild) Pelican Waters Village Pty Ltd v Pelican Waters Village Residents Association Directional Hearing was held in Sydney on Tuesday, 8th February 2011, before Registrar, Mr C Brown.

The receipt of a letter from our operator's Solicitor (Gladsons Lawyers) on the 3rd February requested that we agree to have the Directional Hearing which was set down for the 8th February postponed for a period of six weeks, supposedly to allow us sufficient time to prepare our case. Our legal representative, Peter Hill was opposed to that suggestion and was able to convince Gladsons to not object to the matter proceeding as soon as possible.

As a consequence when the matter was called before the Registrar there was agreement between the legal representatives from both sides that the matter be dealt with at the earliest opportunity available to the Court.

The matter has been set down for a Hearing (full day) on Monday, 14th March 2011 at the John Maddison Tower, 86 Goulburn Street, Sydney.

At the Directional Hearing our legal representative, Peter Hill and I were supported by 36 residents from various villages around Sydney and the Central Coast, this number include the President, the Secretary and two of the Committee of the RVRA. This support was much appreciated. The Court Room was overflowing as all the seating was taken by residents and the waiting legal profession who were also having matters dealt with as set down for Mention had to stand in a very crowded Court Room until their matters were called and dealt with.

As the District Court rulings, unlike the CTTT, sets "precedent at law" there appears to be a great deal of interest in the outcome of this matter. An outcome that is favourable to the Pelican Waters Village residents will prove to be beneficial to retirement village residents throughout the State. Consequently an outcome favourable to Landbuild will no doubt be used by NSW operators as a precedent to restrict the information detail supplied in the presentation of proposed budgets.

I am confident that we have a strong case and have hope of a favourable outcome on the 14th.

Any support by way of letters and emails similar to those received by the RVRA leading up to the Directional Hearing, and in particular attendance on the 14th by our fellow residents from villages within convenient travelling distance of Sydney will be greatly appreciated.

Jack Clarke - 8/02/11

In a phone call that day Jack and Peter discussed the additional documentation that might be required. Additionally the need to keep the campaign of letters to the RVRA and the media would not do any harm as Jack was sure that the RVRA web site on which the various correspondence etc. was listed and detailed was being monitored by various senior Landbuild management. Peter suggested that it might be necessary for Jack, within a week or so, to travel down to his office to personally discuss the issues of the case.

On the 23rd February Jack received the following email from Peter Hill:

Dear Jack,

We have been reviewing all of the material provided by you in relation to the forthcoming appeal. We have also received a list of documents from Gladsons (which is attached) who are preparing an appeal book consistent with the Court's earlier orders.

Can I have you review the list Gladsons have supplied to see if there are any glaring absences, or any documents that were presented that are not in this list. There are some amendments that we will require from Gladsons. The Gladsons list looks pretty comprehensive, though we feel there may have been documents that were tendered at the hearing that were not in the list, but you will need to confirm this.

There are matters Jack that I will need you to undertake some work:

a) Can you provide to me a short written chronological history in very simple terms of what the operator provided when they first tabled the budget (and I would like you to attach the information for both the insurance item and corporate recharge) and then subsequently as you questioned the items, the material that was forthcoming. This will turn out to be quite an important issue in the Appeal, because on what I can see, the insurance cover information was not provided to the residents at all (and only in the attachment to the witness statement of Pierce Burken, once proceedings were on foot), whilst the corporate recharge material included initially the proposed annual budget (with attachment 2 and statement of proposed expenditure- your B1 and B2) and later the

"Corporate Recharge Exposition". I need to know the timing of the production of all of this, because I strongly believe that it will help your case. You see our case is built on the lack of transparency by the operator in providing information for the Committee to make an informed decision. The reality was that even at the hearing, the Operator was continuing to produce information on the run to justify the expense. It seems to me also that the Corporate Recharge Exposition later provided by the operator (and I need to know at what point in the process it was provided) was the first time the Residents heard of the 75% discount. (i.e. only 25% of these costs were being required by the operator to be paid);

b) I need to gain a better understanding of the standard departure arrangements under the pro form leases that were before the Tribunal. It looks like a resident receives back their deposit paid to the trustee and any residue from their upfront rental sum. Can you confirm if this is correct?

c) By the look of it, there is no capital gain sharing? Is this the present situation still in the village?

d) Did you ever obtain the actual insurance policy from the Operator?

e) Can you provide a copy of the Residents Application to the Tribunal?

f) Would you also be able to provide a copy of the Parliamentary Report referenced in the affidavit of Robert McTavish if you have it.

Jack what I would like to do is give you a telephone call shortly to clarify a number of issues prior to you journeying down and it will thereby make your time more productive.

I attach our costs agreement. It will be necessary for you to sign this. Obviously, Landbuilds are funding the costs up to an amount of $50,000 and we believe that this will be sufficient to run the appeal. We will be contacting Gladsons to organise the process for our accounts to be forwarded to them once you have approved these. Shortly, we will be forwarding to you our first account.

I will call you later today to discuss.

Many thanks.

Kind regards,
Peter Hill

Jack replied, "We are working on your requests and I will be meeting with the Sub-Committee on Friday morning. We should be able to get most of it to you on Friday afternoon or Monday morning at the latest. Attached is a copy of the 2005 report to Parliament regarding the proposed change to the Retirement Village Act". Jack also quoted from the *'Office of Fair Trading's Regulatory Impact Statement'* which accompanied the Draft Regulation (September 2009), 8.1 Part 1 – Preliminary (clauses 1 – 9) under the heading *"Assessment of costs and benefits"* the following paragraph appears:

> *The funding split in the Act is based on the premise that the operator owns the capital items in the village and the residents use them. That is, work resulting from the residents' use of the items in the village is able to be funded by residents, and work which replaces, or significantly enhances the value of, the operator's property, or which would need to be done regardless of whether any residents lived in the village, should be paid for by the operator.*

This assessment of 'Who pays for What' by the Office of Fair Trading sums up in simple terms the Residents' and Operator's responsibility as to the funding of the maintenance of capital items.

Over the next two weeks Jack, Bob and Shirley were able to forward to Peter Hill all of the information he had requested. At the last meeting Jack, Bob and Shirley had prior to the District Court Hearing on the 14th March it was agreed that they had done the best that they could have in preparation for the case and that it was now up to Peter Hill and the Judge.

On the 11th March the legal representatives of both the Plaintiff, (Pelican Waters Pty Ltd) and the Defendant, (Pelican Waters Residents Association) sent their submissions to the District Court. This is required in order for the Judge to familiarise himself with the basics of the case prior to the Hearing.

Chapter 13

Plaintiff's (Pelican Waters Pty Ltd) Submission to District Court

The operator's submission was as follows:

> **Pelican Waters Village Pty Ltd V Pelican Waters Village Residents' Association**
>
> **District Court of NSW at Sydney, Case Number 2010/999999**
>
> **Outline of submissions of the plaintiff:**

Introduction

1. The plaintiff ('the Operator") is the operator of Pelican Waters Retirement Village, a retirement village situated on the Mid North Coast in New South Wales.

2. The defendant ("the Residents") is the residents' association at the village.

3. On 9 December 2009 the CTTT made orders pursuant to the *Retirement Villages Act 1999* (NSW) ("RVA") excluding certain items (recurrent charges and insurance) from being included in the budget for Pelican Waters Retirement Village for the financial year 2010/2011

4. The matter came before the CTTT as a result of both parties filing applications seeking that the CTTT determine

the dispute that had arisen between the parties as regards the inclusion of the items in the budget.

5. The Operator brings these proceedings by way of appeal of the decision of the CTTT.

Legal Issues Raised On Appeal

6. The appeal raises the following legal issues:

I The interpretation of the applicable *Retirement Villages Regulation 2009* (NSW) ("RV Regulation") provisions regarding the permissibility of including head office "corporate recharge" items in an annual budget. This directs attention to the precise terms of the RV Regulations and the purpose of the RVA and RV Regulation.

II The failure to consider material evidence, being relevant contractual terms concerning the Operator's entitlement to include "Outgoings" such as insurance in its annual budget.

III The interpretation of s 115 of the CTTT Act and the exercise of discretion by the CTTT under that section.

Summary of Argument

7. The Operator contends the following:

I.   As to the corporate recharge items, the CTTT erred as a matter of law in that it failed to consider whether the budgetary item was a cost or fee *"associated with providing services to residents of the retirement village"* in accordance with the terms of Regulation 26(e) of the RV Regulation, as properly interpreted by reference to its terms and the purpose disclosed by the RVA and the RV Regulation.

II.   As to insurance, the CTTT erred as a matter of law in that it failed to consider whether the insurance was an item within the meaning of the general description of "Outgoing" as defined in the First Schedule to the memorandum of lease, and thereby an item the Operator was entitled to include in its budget.

III.   In respect of each of these errors, had the CTTT applied the correct test, by reference to the evidence, it ought to have found that the corporate recharge entry of $28,594 and the insurance entry of $23,100 were correct entries in the 2010/2011 budget.

IV.   In the alternative, in respect of each of the entries, the CTTT having found that a portion of the budgetary allocation was justifiable the CTTT erred in that it failed to exercise the discretion conferred upon it by S 15(2) of the RVA. It should have either allowed a portion of the budgetary items or alternatively, made other directions or recommendations.

Background

8. The Operator is a wholly owned subsidiary of Dollarvill Limited ("Dollarvill").

9. As at 30 June 2010, Dollarvill operated 30 retirement villages and employed 582 employees across five states.

10. On or about 28 April 2010 the Operator provided to each of the residents of the village the Proposed Annual Budget for the financial year 2010/2011 for the Village, together with a notice of variation of recurrent charges in accordance with the RVA.

11. During May 2010 the residents met, considered and voted on the proposed budget. The Residents notified the Operator that they did not consent to two items in the proposed budget, namely insurance and *"corporate recharges"* as well as to the proposed variation to recurrent charges. The balance of the budget was ultimately approved.

12. The relevant budget entries were $23, 100 for insurance and $28,594 for corporate recharges.

13. In June 2010 both parties filed applications to the CTTT to resolve the dispute.

14. The Operator sought orders under:

I. S 108(1) of the RVA in respect of a proposed variation of recurrent charges,

II. S 115 (1) in respect of the proposed annual budget.

15. The Residents sought an order under s 115(1) that the items be excluded from the 2010/2011 budget and future budgets.

The Retirement Villages Act

16. The objects of the RVA are set out in section 4 in the following terms:

The objects of this Act are:

(a) to set out particular rights and obligations of residents and operators of retirement villages, and

(b) to facilitate the disclosure of information to prospective residents of retirement villages, and(c) to require contracts between residents and operators of retirement villages to contain full details of the rights and obligations of the parties, and

(d) to facilitate resident input, where desired by residents, into the management of retirement villages, and

(e) to establish appropriate mechanisms for the resolution of certain disputes between residents and operators of retirement villages, and (f) to encourage

the retirement village industry to adopt best practice management standards.

17. The RVA is divided into a number of parts and deals with matters such as representations and information about retirement villages entry into retirement villages, village contracts, general Management of retirement villages4, financial management of retirement villages, disputes6, termination of residence contracts and matters relating to vacation of premises.

18. The relationship between residents and operators is governed by the RVA and the village contracts that the parties enter into. The RVA requires that a resident must enter into a village contract prior to occupying residential premises in the village: s 24(1).

Budgets and RecurrentCharges

19. Part 7 of the RVA deals with "Financial Management of Retirement Villages".

20. Part 7 sets out what is required from an operator in respect of the setting of annual budgets for retirement villages and the basis on which certain outgoings, described as "recurrent charges", are to be recovered from residents.

21. A recurrent charge is defined the RVA to mean *"any amount (including rent) payable under a village contract, on a recurrent basis, by a resident of a retirement village"*.

22. A proposed budget and any proposed variation in recurrent charges for the following financial year of a village must be prepared and delivered to each resident in accordance with Part 7 of the RVA.

23. The proposed budget itemizes the way in which the operator proposes to expend the money received by way of recurrent charges required to operate the village. The operating costs of a village are received by way of recurrent charges from the residents of a village during the financial year.

24. If the proposed budget is greater than the previous year's budget the operator will need to collect an increased level of funds from residents by way of variation to the level of recurrent charges to pay for the increased expenditure in the proposed budget. The method of variation of recurrent charges (i.e. by way of fixed or non-fixed formula) is determined by the relevant village contract, in this case it is based on floor area.

25. Section 106 of the RVA deals with increased proposed budgets where there is a proposed increase in recurrent charges exceeding CPI. In this event, the operator is required to provide residents with a copy of the proposed budget and budget notice at least 60 days prior to the commencement of the proposed budget.

26. The residents are then obliged, within 30 days of receiving the documents to do the following:

    I.   Meet, consider and vote on the proposed budget: s114 (4)(a), and

II. Advise the operator that the residents consent or do not consent (as the case may be) to the proposed budget: s 114(4)(b), and

III. If the residents do not consent to the proposed budget - specify the item or items in the proposed budget to which the residents object: s 114(4)(c).

Budgets and Operators of Multiple Villages

27. The RVA recognizes that an operator may run more than one retirement village and conduct other businesses.

28. Section 112(2) of the RVA recognizes that a person who is the operator of more than one retirement village may provide a consolidated budget in relation to any two or more villages concerned with the villages total expenditure, however when providing a budget to residents and former occupants of a particular village, it must include a separate budget for that village.

29. Relevantly, Regulation 17(1)(g) of the Retirement Villages Regulation (RV Regulation"), lists the matters that must be dealt with in the proposed budget and states,

"If any expenditure (proposed or actual) is an apportionment of a total expenditure relating to the village and one or more

other villages or businesses - the method of calculation by which the expenditure is apportioned,".

30. Thus the RVA and RVA regulation contemplate that a head office expense may be apportioned between a particular village and other villages or businesses, however the operator is required to identify and illustrate how the shared expense is apportioned. The Minkara Retirement Village CTTT decisions provide an example in relation to the apportionment of payroll tax.

Village Contracts

31. Before entering into the Village, prospective residents sign an Agreement to Lease. The Agreement to Lease secures a residents' entitlement to reside in the Village in the future. The Agreement to Lease includes the *"matters required to be included in village contracts"* as specified by schedule 2 of the RV Regulation and annexes a copy of the lease.

32. A resident entering into occupation must execute a Lease. The Lease refers to and incorporates a Memorandum to Lease, which is registered upon the residents' entry into the Village.

33. The Agreement to Lease, Lease and Memorandum to Lease comprise the Village Contract, as defined in the RV Act.

34. The Village Contract, subject to the provisions of the RVA sets out the relationship between the parties coming into the Lease, during the term of the Lease and on termination. The Village Contract gives a lessee a residence right in the Village. While living in the Village the resident is required to pay ongoing recurrent charges called 'contributions to outgoings' under the Lease at clause 4. In return the operator provides certain general services to the resident.

35. The Operator is required to provide general services to the residents of the Village, including, as described at clause 20-4 of the Agreement to Lease and clause 13 of the Memorandum of Lease, insurance of the Village to full replacement value and management and administrative services, the costs of which are paid from Outgoings.

36. Clause 20-3 of the Agreement to lease provides that recurrent charges are referred to as "Outgoings" in the Lease and Memorandum of lease.

37. Outgoings are referred to at clause 4 and defined in the First Schedule to the Memorandum as:

> "... the total costs and expenses of the Lessor... (incurred) in the conduct, management and maintenance of Pelican Waters Village and the use and occupation of the same as a high-class retirement village and the use of the Village Centre as a high-class administration and communal centre".

Outgoings are defined to include, (but are not limited to), inter alia,

(iii) all insurance premiums payable by the Lessor in respect of all buildings, fittings, fixtures of Pelican Waters Village for their full insurable reinstatement value; ...

(ix) all reasonable costs (inclusive of wages, superannuation, pension payments and workers compensation insurance) of management, control and administration of Pelican Waters Village. "

38. Residents are obliged to contribute towards the Outgoings of the Village pursuant to clause 4 of the Memorandum to Lease. That contribution is determined by the floor area of a residents' premises as a proportion of the total floor area of the Village (clause 4.1).

39. The maximum specific proportion of the total Outgoings that a resident is required to contribute, by way of recurrent charges, is specified in Item 3 of the Lease.

40. Clause 20-3 of the Agreement to Lease confirms that any increase in Outgoings will be limited to the residents' share of the actual operating costs of the Village. This is equivalent, for the purposes of the RVA, to a non-fixed formula for determining recurrent charges.

Right of Appeal

41. An appeal from a decision of the CTTT is governed by section 67 of the CTTT Act, which is relevantly in the following terms:

(1) If, in respect of any proceedings, the Tribunal decides a question with respect to a matter of law, a party in the proceedings who is dissatisfied with the decision may, subject to this section appeal to the District Court against the decision.

(2) An appeal is to be made in accordance with the rules of the District Court. The rules of the District Court may provide that an appeal (or such classes of appeal as may be specified in the rules) may be made only with the leave of the Court.

(3) After deciding the question the subject of such an appeal, the District Court may, unless it affirms the decision of the Tribunal on the question: (a) make such order in relation to the proceedings in which the question arose as, in its opinion, should have been made by the Tribunal. or

(b) Remit its decision on the question to the Tribunal and order a rehearing of the proceedings by the Tribunal.

(4) If such a rehearing is held, the Tribunal is not to proceed in a manner, or make an order or a decision, that is inconsistent with the decision of the District Court remitted to the Tribunal.

42. The scope of what may constitute a decision of a question with respect to a matter of law was most recently considered by the High Court in *Kostas v HIA Insurance Services Pty Limited",

43. The High Court interpreted s 67 broadly. It held that the words *"question with respect to a matter of law are wide enough to encompass* a *question of mixed law and fact'.*

44. The Court declined to adopt the *"taxonomy"* sought to be identified by Basten JA in the Court of Appeal that appeals under s 67(1) are *"restricted in some way to legal error'* by reference to particular categories of appeal provisions.

45. The Court held that:

"The language of the statute must be the relevant starting point not a *taxonomy which seeks to reduce a wide variety of statutory provisions to* a *few discrete categories.*

46. It also held:

Whether there was no evidence to support a factual finding is a *question of law, not of fact*

A tribunal that decides a *question of fact when there is "no evidence" in support of the finding makes an error of law. What amounts to material that could support* a *factual finding is ultimately* a *question for judicial decision. It is a question of law".*

209

The CTTT Hearing and Decision

47. The CTTT hearing took place on 8 November 2010 at Port Macquarie.

48. The parties were not legally represented. Both parties provided written submissions and other documentation. In addition the parties relied on affidavits and/or witness statements. All the material that was before the CTTT is contained in exhibit JS1 to the affidavit of Jessica Carly Smith dated 8 March 2011. There was no transcript of the proceedings before the CTTT.

49. The CTTT delivered its decision by way of written reasons dated 9 December 2010.

50. As noted above, the Operator sought orders under sections 108 and of the RVA. The residents sought an order under section 115. As noted by the CTTT at paragraph [76] of the determination, section 115(7) provides that if the CTTT receives an application under s 115 at the same time as it has before it an application under s 108 it must first make a determination of any application under s 115.

51. The principal order of the CTTT was that pursuant to s 115(2)(e) an order was made that the line item of *"insurance"* in the sum of $23, 100 and the line item of *"corporate recharges"* in the sum of $28,594 are both excluded from the budget for the Village for the financial year 2010/2011.

52. As to the corporate recharge issue, the CTTT identified the *"fundamental issue for determination"* as to whether the amounts charged are *"costs or fees associated with providing services to residents of the retirement village"*, by reference to Regulation 26(e).

53. It was contended on behalf of the Operator that the budget entry related to five areas of head office operation that were associated with the provision of services to the village. If the matters were not dealt with by head office the village would need to employ people to undertake the relevant tasks (at greater expense). Detail at the hearing was provided as to how the proportion of charges was allocated to the Village. It was submitted that the corporate recharge items and the manner of allocation was in accordance with Regulations 17(1)(g) and 26(e) of the RV Regulation.

54. The CTTT excluded the corporate recharge items from the budget. It accepted that some of the functions performed by employees the subject of the budget entry *"provide* a *direct or indirect service to residents:"*, but found there was *"insufficient information available ... to draw the conclusion that the whole of the sum that was apportioned to Pelican Waters Village as corporate recharge was in fact for expenses associated with the provision of services to the village"*

55. As to the insurance item, it was argued on behalf of the Operator that it was entitled to have the insurance item included as a

211

budget item by reference to s 100 of the RVA and the First Schedule to the Memorandum of Lease.

56. The CTTT found that the relevant risks being insured were identified in the following terms:

- Material damage to property insured

- Consequential loss (business interruption), gross profit, payroll, professional fees, claims preparation

- Cover for infectious or contagious diseases, vermin, pests or defective sanitary arrangements, food or drink poisoning, murder or suicide, works of art, antiques or curios, cash in safe or transit, replacement of records, loss of land value, etc.

57. It was held that

"Clearly, the insurance cover effected by the respondent goes far beyond the scope of that provided for under s 100. Items such as loss of profits, insurance of works of art not located on the premises, cash in transit, etc. are not within the contemplation of the obligation to imposed under s100'

58. The CTTT then considered whether there is a contractual obligation for residents to pay additional insurance charges by reference to clause (iii) of The First Schedule of the Memorandum To Lease which stipulates that Outgoings shall include,

"All insurance premiums payable by the Lessor in respect of all buildings fitting fixtures of Pelican Waters Village their full insurable reinstatement value against fire flood lightning storm and tempest and in respect of insurance of Pelican Waters Village against such other risks (referable to Pelican Waters Village or the Lessor in relation to the Lessor's ownership or interest in Pelican Waters Village) as the Council Of Management may deem necessary or desirable".

59. The CTTT determines the matter at paragraph [58]:

"There is simply no evidence that the Council of Management has considered the issue. Even if there had been evidence of deeming by the Council of Management, it would still have left the question unanswered as to whether all of the risks insured are "referable to Pelican Waters Village" as required to schedule 1 of the Memorandum of Lease".

60. The CTTT concludes, in respect of the insurance issue:

"However, I am not satisfied that the whole of the portion of the premium attributed to Pelican Waters Village by the operator is payable by the residents under the Act or pursuant to their individual contracts".

Errors of The CTTT

The Corporate Recharge

213

61. In order to understand the proper basis of the inclusion of corporate recharge it is necessary to consider all relevant regulations, not merely 26(e).

62. Relevantly, Regulation 17 deals with matters that must be dealt with in a proposed annual budget.

63. Regulation 17(1)(g) states that one of the matters that must be dealt with in the proposed annual budget is,

"if any expenditure (proposed or actual) is an apportionment of a total expenditure relating to the village and one or more other villages or businesses-the method or calculation by which the expenditure is apportioned".

64. Regulation 17(2) states:

"If the annual budget includes any costs associated with the operator's head office or any management or administration fees, these are to be broken down to show the goods and services to which they relate and the approximate cost of those goods and services."

65. Regulation 26 identifies matters that cannot be financed by way of recurrent charges. Pursuant to Regulation 26(e) costs associated with the operator's head office or management or administration fees must not be financed by way of recurrent charges *"unless the costs or fees are associated with providing services to residents of the retirement village".*

66. Regulations 17(1)(g), 17(2) and 26(e) state the basis on which recurrent charges are to be included in a proposed annual budget and the manner they are included.

67. The correct interpretation of these regulations is a purposive one, as required by section 33 of the Interpretation Act 1987 (NSW), which provides:

"In the interpretation of a provision of an Act or statutory rule, a construction that would promote the purpose or object underlying the Act or statutory rule (whether or not that purpose or object is expressly stated in the Act or statutory rule or, in the case of a statutory rule, in the Act under which the rule was made) shall be preferred to a construction that would not promote that purpose or object."

68. The proper approach is relevantly described in the judgment of the High Court in *Cooper Brookes (Wollongong) PIL v FCT22*, by Mason and Wilson JJ in the following terms:

"The fundamental object of statutory construction in every case is to ascertain the legislative intention by reference to the language of the instrument viewed as a whole. But in performing that task the courts look to the operation of the statute according to its terms and to legitimate aids to construction...

Quite obviously questions of degree arise. If the choice is between two strongly competing interpretations, as we have said, the advantage may lie with that which produces the fairer and more convenient operation so long as it conforms to the legislative intention. If, however, one interpretation has a powerful advantage in ordinary meaning and grammatical sense, it will only be displaced if its operation is perceived to be unintended."

69. The key issue, identified by the CTTT, is what is meant by the phrase *"associated with providing services to residents of the retirement village"* as used in RV Regulation 26(e).

70. This phrase, however, must be considered against a background of the following matters:

I. The RVA and RV Regulation disclose an intention to permit operators of multiple villages to include in their budgets head office expenses where they are associated with provision of service to a village or villages,

II. The budget, being prospective, is necessarily for future estimated costs.

III. There must be transparency in respect of the method or calculation by which the expenditure is apportioned as between villages,

IV. The budget must disclose a breakdown of the particular goods and services to which the fees relate,

V. The breakdown is provided on an approximate basis.

71. The intent disclosed by Regulation 26(e) is to distinguish between head office costs that are related to the provision of services to villages and those that are not. The primary purpose is to establish a general rule that head office costs (for example in the nature of sales and marketing, business development and the like) are excluded but that costs associated with provision of services to villages - being costs if the village were stand alone would be incurred by the village and thereby properly included in the budget - are carved out of the exclusion.

72 In all the circumstances, a sensible purposive interpretation of Regulation 26(e) is that the operator must show that relevant services have a rational connection to the village. Conversely, it cannot reasonably be the purpose of the Regulation to require the operator to descend to a degree of specific detail in its budget so that it must demonstrate that the totality of expenses apportioned resulted in particular services to residents of the Village.

73. Significantly, the regulation deals with costs or expenses *"associated with"* the provision of services and not for example, costs or expenses directly related to or solely for the provision of services. In *Hutchinson 3G v City of Mitcham,* the High Court considered a regulation that stipulated that a development must be "used for or associated with" the supplying, converting, transforming or controlling of electricity. The Court held:

"The apparent width of the phrase "used for or associated with" in par (a)(ii) of Schedule 14A suggests a nexus between a proposed development and the purpose of supplying, converting, transforming or controlling electricity which is not so stringent as to require that that purpose be the sole purpose of the proposed development."

74. *"Associated with"* is analogous to *"in connection with"* - there must be a rational connection or nexus. It is not the language of a provision requiring narrow interpretation. It is a phrase recognized by the High Court as having *"apparent width"*.

75. The CTTT erred because it failed to interpret regulation 26(e) in a purposive manner as disclosed by and in accordance with its terms.

76. The relevant portion of the determination of the CTTT is set out at paragraphs [66] - [70] of the decision.

77. The CTTT, while accepting that the various items of corporate recharge relate to functions that *"do in fact provide a direct or indirect service to the residents"* found that *"there is insufficient information to determine that all the expenses that were apportioned were associated with the provision of services to residents"*.

78. The CTTT erred in arriving at this conclusion.

79. The evidence that was before the CTTT demonstrated that that the expenses were associated with the provision of services to residents.

80. The Operator's evidence identified each of the areas to which the fees related - human resources, payroll, finance, information technology and finance. Mr Burken's statement provided an explanation as to the association with the provision of services to the Village.

81. Human resources is dealt with at paragraphs [16]-[22]. There is a description of the function of the head office human resources division. At paragraphs 19 - 20 there is a description as to how the services are associated with the Village. The matters coordinated by the HR department relate to all the villages, including the Village. At paragraph 21 the observation is made that if the Village were stand alone *"it would need some form of administration process to address all aspects as dealt with by the human resources department of Dollarvill"*. Paragraph 22 states the basis of allocation amongst the villages.

82. The role of payroll and its necessity and connection with the Village is established at paragraphs [23]-[26] of Mr Burken's statement. The manner of allocation is set out in paragraph [27J.

83. Similarly, with finance, there is a description of the functions performed by the finance staff at head office that relate to all

villages including the Village - see in particular paragraph [30]. The basis for allocation is set out at paragraph [31].

84. Mr Burken describes the level of information technology operations across the villages including the Village at paragraphs [34]-[37], including with reference to the benefit accruing to residents:

   "The ability to retain information electronically and be able to retrieve it efficiently is a necessary service with respect to resident amenity as information relating to interactions with residents both in terms of accounts, care needs, support needs and file notes, which are an important part of a residents' history at a village and accordingly, need to be maintained".

85. At paragraph [40] of his affidavit Mr Burken sets out details of administrative functions performed by head office staff associated with the provision of services to villages, including the Village.

86. The evidence of Mr Burken regarding the association of the charges with services to the village is corroborated by the statement of Rochelle Train, the Village Manager at the village.

87. Ms Stephenson's statement demonstrates how each of the head office charges is associated with the provision of services to the Village - with respect to financial information technology and human resources'". She sets out in detail her responsibilities for resident welfare and upkeep of the Village, continuous

improvement, financial management and legislative compliance34, stating that her functions are performed by her relying upon the head office resources of information technology, accounting, administration support, payroll and human resources.

88. The statement of Amam Lam, Dollarvill financial controller, describes the methodology for calculation of the corporate recharge - in specific terms this is set out in paragraph [17]. The method of allocation is set out in paragraph [25].

89. The CTTT erred because it failed to apply Regulation 26(e) in accordance with its terms and its purpose.

90. The error in the approach of the CTTT is laid bare by the findings in paragraph 68 of the decision, when after reference to the functions of the finance division there are the following findings:

"I think it is self-evident that many of these functions do in fact provide a direct or indirect service to the residents. Some do not. For example, how could the attendance to a query raised by a supplier to Dollarvill Ltd be interpreted as a provision of a service to the residents of Pelican Waters Village? There is some merit in the inclusion of expenses from the finance division, but there is insufficient information to determine that all the expenses that were apportioned were associated with the provision of services to the residents".

91. It is contrary to the terms and purpose of the RVA and RV Regulation to require the Operator to demonstrate that the expenses are for the *"provision of a service to the residents of Pelican Waters Village"*. This approach fails to give operation to the words *"associated with"*. It is also contrary to the import of the RVA and the RV Regulation that contemplate a process whereby the operators of multiple villages can legitimately and sensibly allocate head office costs amongst their villages in their respective budgets. It would be counter to the purpose of the RVA and RV Regulation to require the Operator to undertake a work intensive process to justify certain budgetary items. Such a process would be costly and possibly something that would be liable to be passed on to residents.

92. It cannot have been the intention of the provisions that an operator must, in order to justify a budget item, demonstrate in precise terms that each of the expenses related to a service to the benefit of the residents of the specific village - yet this was the approach taken by the CTTT. Such an approach is onerous on the operator and would require an unrealistic degree of detail in budget preparation. It is particularly unrealistic bearing in mind the budget is prospective and is (as acknowledged in the Regulation) an estimate of expenses broken down on an approximate basis.

93. Critically, no attempt was made by the CTTT to assess whether the relevant services were *"associated with"* the provision of

services to the Village; that is to say, there was no assessment as to whether there was a rational connection between the expenses and the provision of services. There was no attempt to give meaning to the words "associated with". The CTTT in all the circumstances should have allowed all of the corporate recharge expense as it satisfied the tests and obligations under the RVA and RV Regulation.

AlternativeCase: Error in Orders Made

95. As noted above, the CTTT found that at least a portion of disputed items are costs or fees associated with providing services to residents of the retirement village.

96. In the circumstances, having made this finding, the CTTT erred in rejecting the budget items in total.

97. The reasoning of the CTTT appeared to be that the Operator was required to prove it was entitled to include the items in the budget on an all or nothing basis. No such test is imposed by the RVA.

98. Section 115 provides the CTTT with a discretion to allow a portion of the budget items section (115(2)(f)) or alternatively make orders pursuant to 115(2)(b) and (c).

99. Having found that at least a portion of the corporate recharge items were within the scope of the exception to Regulation 26 the CTTT erred in the outright rejection of the items.

100. The CTTT erred in failing to turn its mind to the exercise of the discretion conferred by section 115(2). Whilst s 115(2) is reproduced in the decision there is no indication that all its terms have been considered. Its terms contemplate that the CTTT may make directions to facilitate agreement between the parties, recommendations concerning the expenses and also allowing a portion of expenses claimed (115(2)(f)).

101. There being a finding that a portion of the expenses were within the scope of the exception to regulation 26(e), it cannot be consistent with the purpose disclosed by s 115(2) to simply reject the budget entry in total. Section 115 does not require the CTTT to reject a budgetary item on an all or nothing basis. The discretion conferred on the CTTT by its terms discloses a purpose of permitting a portion of budgetary items where appropriate, whether by partial allowance, or further directions between the parties.

102. The CTTT had a discretion which it was required to act upon by reason of the terms of s 115(2).

103. There was an error by the CTTT in failing to turn its mind to the exercise of the discretion. In its dismissal of the budget

item in total it failed to have regard to a relevant matter - namely the discretion conferred by s 115(2).

104. Put alternatively, the CTTT erred in the exercise of its discretion because when making its ordered pursuant to s 115(2) it failed to take into account a material consideration (its finding that a portion of the expenses were associated with the provision of services to residents of the Village) or acted upon a wrong principle (its failure to consider the discretion available to it). There being such an error, in conformity with *House v The King36*, the determination ought to be reviewed and the appellate Court may *"exercise its own discretion in substitution for [the CTTT if it has the materials for doing so"*.

105. The effect of the decision is that the CTTT found that a proportion of the corporate recharge expenses were legitimate to pass on to residents but yet it was not permitted to include those expenses in its budget.

106. If, contrary to the primary submissions above, the Court does not consider the Operator has established it is entitled to include the whole of the corporate recharge expenses in its budget for 2010/2011, the issue properly remaining for determination is the proportion that it is entitled to include in its budget. In the current case the Court may consider there is insufficient material to allow it to determine this issue. It is open to the Court to make orders pursuant to s 115 (2)(b) and (c),

either independent of or in addition to an order for a rehearing pursuant to sections 67(3) and (4) if the CTTT Act.

The Insurance Issue

107. The evidence before the CTTT of the insurance policy in respect of which contribution was sought was annexure A to the affidavit of Mr Pierce Burken, the general manager for operations for Dollarvill38. This document was a quotation from Dollarvill's broker *"in relation to the facility if it were a stand alone facility"*.

108. The quotation describes the policy as an "Industrial Special Risks Policy", with "Interest Insured" as "Material Damage" and "Consequential Loss (Business Interruption)". In addition, there are policy endorsements for matters including fusion, infectious or contagious diseases, vermin and the other matters identified by the CTTT at [55] of the decision.

109. Section 100 of the RV Act provides: *(2) The village must have insurance that:*

(a) covers the following:

(i) damage,

(ii) costs incidental to the reinstatement or replacement of insured buildings,

(iii) public liability, and

(b) provides for the reinstatement of property to its condition when new.

110. Pursuant to the Memorandum to Lease the Operator is entitled to pass on the expense of *"Outgoings"* to its residents.

111. The term *"Outgoings"* is defined to mean *"the total cost of all outgoings costs and expenses of the lessor now or hereafter properly and reasonably assessed charged or chargeable paid or payable or otherwise incurred upon or in respect of the whole of Pelican Waters Village and the Village Centre or upon the Lessor in relation thereto or in the conduct management and maintenance of Pelican Waters Village and the use and occupation of the same as a high class retirement village and the Village Centre as a high class administrative and communal centre".*

112. Clause (iii) of The First Schedule of the Memorandum To Lease makes specific reference to insurance but it is expressed as an example of an Outgoing and in terms where it does not *"limit the generality of the foregoing Outgoings".*

113. The CTTT confined its consideration in respect of the memorandum to Lease to the terms of Clause (iii) of the First Schedule. It failed to have regard to the entirety of the First Schedule and in particular the description of "Outgoings", in respect of which the various specific matters referred to

(including insurance) are expressed in terms *"Without limiting the generality of the foregoing Outgoings"*.

114. In the circumstances the CTTT erred in that it asked the wrong question. It misdirected itself in that it limited its analysis as to whether the insurance policy fitted within the terms of Clause (iii) rather than whether it was an Outgoing pursuant to the First Schedule. There was a failure to consider relevant evidence, being the principal provisions dealing with "Outgoings" in the Memorandum to Lease.

115. The cost of the insurance policy comfortably fits within the definition of "Outgoings". It is a cost incurred *"in respect of the whole of Pelican Waters Village and the Village Centre or upon the Lessor in relation thereto or in the conduct management and maintenance of Pelican Waters Village and the use and occupation of the same"*.

116. Had the policy not been taken out by Dollarvill it would need to have been taken out as a stand-alone policy at greater expense." Mr Burken's statement also describes the formula for allocation of the insurance policy cost to a particular village. The Village property value is divided by the total Dollarvill property value. This percentage is then multiplied by the insurance premium to derive the Village insurance premium allocation or component. The property valuations are undertaken independently every six months.

117. There is further justification for the inclusion of the insurance premium in the budget by reason of clause 13.4 of the Memorandum to Lease which provides that the Lessor will maintain insurance policies insuring the Village *"for its full insurable value against loss or damage by fire earthquake storm tempest damage by aircraft and other usual insurable risks".*

118. The CTTT erred in failing to consider whether the policy came within the scope of clause 13.4. The quotation provided is for what is described as an Industrial Special Risks ("ISR") policy. This is a well known form of insurance policy. There is no reason to regard the insurance as anything other than insurance for the *"usual insurable risks".* An ISR policy is not an unusual or exotic policy of insurance. It is the type of policy that would be reasonably expected for a going concern such as a retirement village.

119. In addition to its error in failing to direct itself as to whether the insurance premium was an "Outgoing" within the terms of Schedule 1 to the Memorandum of Lease, the CTTT erred in failing to find that the policy was taken out pursuant clause 13.4.

120. The result of such consideration would lead to the same conclusion - namely, that the allocation premium is an Outgoing pursuant to Schedule 1 of the Memorandum of Lease.

121. Furthermore, as with the corporate recharge items, the CTTT erred in its failure to exercise its discretion under section 115(2) of the RV Act in making an order that there is to be no inclusion at all of this item in the proposed annual budget.

Alternative Case; Error in Orders made

122. The CTTT expressly found that a portion of the insurance cover comes within the scope of section 100 and, implicitly, the Memorandum of Lease.

123. However the premium attributed to the Village in the proposed budget was totally rejected because the CTTT was not satisfied that the whole of the portion of premium attributed to the Village was payable by the residents under the RVA or pursuant to their individual contracts.

124. This is not a proper basis for the rejection of the entirety of the insurance item in the budget. Such a test is not prescribed by the RVA or the contracts. This approach, which is tantamount to imposing an onus on the Operator to prove its case on an all or nothing basis, is not supported by the provisions of the RVA.

125. It is also inconsistent with the discretion conferred by section 115(2) which provides the CTTT may make orders including allowing a portion of item in the budget, giving directions to the parties to facilitate agreement concerning the proposed expenditure and make recommendations to the parties about the proposed expenditure.

126. Having found that a portion of the insurance cover was within the scope of section 100 and, implicitly the Memorandum of Lease, the CTTT erred in rejecting the entirety of the insurance item from the proposed budget. It failed to exercise the discretion conferred upon it by s115(2) of the RVA.

127. In similar terms to the corporate recharge, the CTTT's orders give rise to the absurdity that there is a finding that a significant proportion of the insurance cost is properly recoverable, yet the Operator is not entitled to any recovery in the budget.

128. As with the corporate recharge item it is open to the Court to make orders pursuant to s 115 (2)(b) and (c), either independent of or in addition to an order for a rehearing pursuant to sections 67(3) and (4) if the CTTT Act.

Conclusion

129. By reason of the primary submissions herein the Operator contends for orders in accordance with orders 2,3,4 and 6 of the Summons dated 23 December 2010.

130. If the Operator is not successful in its primary submissions, it submits that the appropriate course is for orders to be made for a rehearing with a view to determining the portion of each of the expenses that may be included as a budget entry. To this end the Court may also make orders pursuant to sections 115(2)(b) and (c) of the RVA.

131. In the event the Operator is successful in this appeal it does not seek an order for costs.

11 March 2011

Ivan Gittoes   Counsel for the plaintiff

Phillip Street, Sydney NSW 2000

Chapter 14

Defendant's (Pelican Waters Residents Association) Submission to District Court

The residents' submission was as follows:

District Court of NSW

Plaintiff :   Pelican Waters Village Pty Ltd

Defendant: Pelican Waters Village Residents Association

Case Number 2010/999999

Hearing Date 14th March 2011

Outline of Submissions for the Defendant-   Pelican Waters Residents Committee

1.   Introduction

1.1   Before the Court is an appeal from a decision of Tribunal Member Mr Jeffrey Jones in the Consumer, Trader and Tenancy Tribunal (the CTTT) disallowing the line items of insurance and "corporate recharge" items in the 2010-2011 budget for the Pelican Waters Retirement Village (Village).

1.2   The Court must first decide whether leave to appeal from Mr Jones's decision be granted. The Defendant says no to this question and that leave to appeal be denied.

1.3   If the Court be against the Defendant on this it must then decide whether or not to grant the appeal.   It is the defendant's submission that the appeal be dismissed.

2.   Context of CTTT's Decision

2.1   In the course of deciding these legal questions on appeal, the context of the issues before the CTTT, as presented in the evidence, are particularly instructive.

2.2   The village comprises 124 independent living units with 160 residents in total residing in the village. The village operates as an independent living unit with user pay services (see witness statement of Rochelle Train at Tab 8). Dollarvill Limited acquired and took over the management of the village in August 2006 (witness statement of Roy Dunlop at Tab "H").

2.3   The Plaintiff is a wholly owned subsidiary of Dollarvill Limited ("Dollarvill"). The Plaintiff is part of a very large corporate structure.   As at 30th June 2010 Dollarvill was operating 30 retirement villages and 367 residential aged care beds across five States. Dollarvill's primary function is to operate the group's retirement village portfolio, its nursing home and low care lodges and to continue to further develop, acquire and build retirement village and aged care portfolios (see witness statement of Pierce Burken at Tab 5).

2.4   Residents who reside in the village do not own the freehold in their home, but occupy their residence under a long term (99 year) registered lease. The entry costs are significant and likewise, the financial imposts on departure charged by the operator to the vacating resident. On entry to Pelican Waters Retirement Village, residents are required to pay a non-interest bearing redeemable deposit (it is redeemable on vacation) as well as a large rent in advance amount which is deducted at 5% per year up to a maximum of 5 years. Hence, after 5 years in the village and on vacation or departure, residents are required to pay 25% which swallows up the rent in advance amount and if they stay a shorter period, then they receive back any residue remaining of the upfront rent component. Residents are also required to share the capital gain with the operator on any sale of the residence to a new resident.

In addition, during their occupation, the resident must meet monthly general service charges levied by the operator (see Tab 3A, 3B & 3C detailing lease arrangements). The financial penalties to residents on vacation of their residence is described under the Act as a "departure fee". This fee has traditionally been applied by operators in the industry as a deferred management cost to recover costs (obviously with a margin) that could not otherwise be recovered by the operator through recurrent charges.

2.5   Now under the *Retirement Villages Act 1999* (the Act), each year the operator is required to present to residents a budget of proposed expenditure for approval. This budget sets the scene for the amount of monthly recurrent general service charges residents are required to pay. As a general proposition, under the Act, the operator is responsible for meeting capital replacement costs in the village, whilst residents meet the costs of capital maintenance. The approval of the annual budget is critical to the determination of how much residents will be required to pay in their monthly charges for the forthcoming year.

2.6   When Dollarvill took over the village in August 2006, residents were informed that many benefits would accrue arising from the breadth and scale of the new owner's operations. These included savings in the budget items presented to residents each year. Dollarvill's first budget was for the year 2007-2008 and it was in that year that the concept of corporate recharge costs were introduced (see witness statement of Roy Dunlop at Tab H). But we see from the evidence of Robert McTavish for the residents before the Tribunal (see Tab Q2) that there was a growing practice amongst operators for such "head office" costs of very large operators being apportioned   to villages for payment by residents through the recurrent charge process and that such costs were more closely associated with the running of their business and breadth of operations and not the provision of services to residents. Corporate recharge costs had not arisen in the past before the takeover by

236

Dollarvill of the Pelican Waters Village. At Tab 7 of the operator's evidence before the Tribunal we see the witness statement of Rochelle Train who asserted in relation to the corporate recharge costs that if these charges and the services provided consequentially to the village were not undertaken, as Village Manager, she would not be able to provide all of the required services to the village nor efficiently undertake her functions. Ms Train's evidence sat in contradiction to that of Mr McTavish (at Tab Q2) for the residents committee, that it was only after the takeover by Dollarvill that these wider corporate charges became an issue in the budget and by implication, the village was being run efficiently in the period before without them. Mr McTavish also asserts in his affidavit that much of the composition of these head office costs were either more closely aligned with the normal operating costs to run a business than the provision of a service to residents at the actual village or were picked up in other line items of the budget dealing with the payment of staff salaries for staff based at the village and through the property and other capital maintenance line items in the budget.

2.7 Mr McTavish's observation in his affidavit before the Tribunal (at Tab Q2) of the growing trend of large operators to flow through wider corporate operating costs had also caught the gaze of the legislature. Prior to the passing by Parliament of the 2008 amendments to the Act, the legislation was reviewed by the Office of Fair Trading and a report was prepared in March 2005.

The Report noted the concern of residents in the industry of the practice of including in the operating budget, expenses unrelated to the operation of the village, which included costs of unrelated businesses or items, such as management fees. At recommendation 26 of the Report it recommended "that expenses unrelated to the operation or administration of a village (such as management fees) be prohibited from inclusion in a village budget".

2.8   The second reading speech to the introduction of the 2008 amendments spoke of the bills commitment to ensuring appropriate consumer protection for a vulnerable segment of the population - that is persons who live in retirement villages. The Regulations to the 2008 amendments (Retirement Villages Regulation 2009) included specific additions to address these very questions of corporate recharge items by requiring the annual budget to break down these costs so as to show the goods and services to which they related (Reg 17 (2)) and inserted provisions which specifically excluded costs associated with the operator's head office or management or administration fees unless these costs or fees were associated with providing services to residents of the retirement village. These provisions were at the heart of Mr Jones's decision on the corporate re-charge items that are now before the Court on appeal.

2.9   When the line items in the budget of insurance and corporate recharge amounts came before the CTTT as the basis of the rejection of the 2010-2011 budget by residents, it was apparent to Tribunal Member Jones that the level of detail provided by the operator in relation to supporting information was severely lacking. At paragraph 44 on page 10 of the Member's judgement Mr Jones states,

"It is asserted by the applicant that there has been a lack of transparency in the process adopted by the respondent during this dispute. The applicant complains that little, if any, information was provided at the time of the notification of the proposed budget to assist residents in identifying the nature and extent of the costs they were being asked to fund. I believe that complaint is valid (the respondent's representative acknowledged at the hearing that the details of the insurance cover had not been provided to the residents and the allocation of corporate recharge costs had been provided during the course of proceedings and not with the proposed budget). .... "

2.10   It is against the backdrop of:

• a very large operator with a significant corporate head office and corporate structure;

• an increasingly more vigilant resident group seeking to ensure value for money in what they were being required to pay for in terms of services received across the village;

- a legislative environment that had seen the need for greater checks and balances for residents in the budgetary process;

- an operator who had a stated goal of growing larger in the retirement village industry;

- an operator, that on their own admission, had provided little information by way of justification for the line items of insurance and corporate recharge costs at the time the budget was presented to residents and indeed thereafter;

that the Tribunal made its decision.

3.   Leave to Appeal be Denied

3.1   Appeals to the District Court from the CTTT are only available on questions of law and the Plaintiff must be granted leave to proceed. To be granted leave, the Plaintiff must establish that they have an arguable case..

3.2   The Defendant submits fundamentally on two grounds that leave to appeal be denied.

3.3   First, the appeal, in reality, lends itself on its grounds to a dissatisfaction with the material findings on the evidence by Mr Jones, and not because of some erroneous or perverse interpretation of the Act. It is dressed up and quaintly characterised, as an appeal based on an erring in law by Mr Jones but at the heart of its plea is a general dissatisfaction with the Member's conclusions.

The arguability with Mr Jones's decision that the Plaintiff has is more appropriately characterised with a dissatisfaction with the Member's findings of fact on the evidence, not on any question of law which must exist to grant leave to appeal being granted. But herein lies the dual problem for the Plaintiff because to appeal on this basis was to petition the CTTT under section 68 of the *Consumer, Trader and Tenancy Tribunal Act 2001* for a re• hearing - grounds which are very limited and in our submission not available though this is the import of their appeal to the District Court. A re-hearing in the CTTT will only be granted if the Chairperson decides that a party has suffered a substantial injustice on the basis that the decision was either not fair or equitable, was against the weight of evidence or new evidence is available that did not exist at the time.

3.4   Second, the interpretation of the relevant sections of the Act by Mr Jones really amount to the most obvious conclusion based on their context and form - it is difficult to envisage any alternative construction. The Member's interpretation of them is neither erroneous nor perverse nor does violence to the content of the legislation as a whole, including the objects of the Act.

3.5   For these reasons, we submit that the Plaintiffs case on Mr Jones's interpretation has little if any arguability and leave to appeal should be denied.

4.   Appeal be Dismissed

4.1   In the event that the Court decides to grant leave to appeal, we submit for the Defendant that the appeal be dismissed. The grounds upon which our client relies also include the reasons upon which we submit that leave to appeal should not be granted, but also others.

Insurance Cover Went Far Beyond What the Act Would Permit

4.2   Section 100 of the Act dealing with insurance changes is straight forward in what it requires an operator to do by way of insurance and the funding of it in the annual budget. The reality of the section is that it is non-contentious in its construction or ambit. The village must have insurance that covers the matters in subsection 2, 3 and 4 and residents can be asked to pay for it.

4.3   The dilemma before Mr Jones was that the policy produced by the operator went well beyond the matters in section 100. The cost was an aggregate one for the breadth of the coverage.

4.4   The further dilemma was that the purported contractual obligation had not been followed by the operator in so far as the extra risks were determined by the Council of Management under the relevant lease. Mr Jones did have regard to the contractual obligations, but found on the evidence that these did not sit comfortably with what had actually occurred. It was the evidence of the operator that was lacking on this issue and whether or not all of the risks were referable to Pelican Waters Village.

4.5   Tribunal Member Jones did touch on the unenforceability of any contractual term that derogated from the Act or Regulations. This was not greatly expanded on by the Member and is dealt with in the Defendants Notice of Contention. In short, the contractual provision relied on by the operator to justify the additional insurance items beyond the matters required by the Act are tantamount to the contracting out of the provisions under section 100 and prohibited by section 199 . They are unenforceable.

4.6   The logical corollary of the Plaintiffs argument in respect of these contractual provisions is that their argument would require residents to pay for whatever the operator believed insurance over the village and the risks it wished to safeguard against was appropriate. These risks, for a very large business, could go well beyond the matters defined in section 100 and on the operator's argument, the residents would be required to approve the budget. They could also be risks not referable to a particular village. This would defeat the checks and balances contained in the Act regarding recurrent charges and abrogate the very specific safeguards in section 100.

Corporate Recharge Costs Lacked Transparency

4.7   The starting point for the Tribunal's reasoning on the corporate recharge cost was the compilation of section 112 and Regulation 26. In the Plaintiff's submission, these provisions were applied correctly.

4.8   As the Tribunal pointed out on page 12 of the judgement: *"The fundamental issue for determination is whether or not the amounts charged under the heading of corporate recharge are costs or fees associated with providing services to residents of the retirement village."*

4.9   The legal construction of this provision is uncontentious, is neither complex nor difficult to surmise as to its meaning and intent. The reality was that the Tribunal did not err at law. They looked at what the operator presented and formed a judgement on the evidence as to whether the charges sought could be justified.

4.10   The reality of the situation is that the complexity did not lie for the Tribunal in the interpretation   of Regulation 26 but in establishing a line of sight between what was being   said were the services being provided by the operator   a nd what the evidence actually showed.

4.11   In short, the methodology produced by the operator,   and we submit, only in readiness   for the   hearing, was a 'black   box'. The Corporate Recharge Exposition statement at Tab 3 F provided a different explanation and discounted the charges on this line item by a factor of 75%. The problem with the operator's calculations is that they were in charge of determining what the discount was in any given budget. For 2010/2011 they identified that it was 75%, but this had no bearing to the checks and balances in the Act. As the operations of the operator   grew over time (which is their stated intention) there   was   no   touchstone or anchor in principle as

244

to what residents would pay. If the Head Office functions grew by a factor of say tenfold unrelated to any of the services in Pelican Waters Village, the methodology for apportionment would simply allocate the cost to the residents. Hardly a fair or just outcome, nor one we submit which is supported by the consumer protection provisions of the Act.

Apportionment of Insurance & Corporate Recharge Costs Was Not Open on the Evidence Nor Sought by the Operator

4.12   The Plaintiff has relied heavily in the grounds of their appeal on the fact that the Tribunal did not apportion those insurance and corporate recharge costs which were allowable under the Act.

4.13   Well firstly, the operator did not seek the Tribunal to do this either in their application nor in their submissions. They ran an 'all or nothing case' in so far as the charges were concerned.

4.14   But, in any event, the problem for the Tribunal was more fundamental. On the evidence, the Member simply could not separate out the insurance costs that were potentially allowable from the aggregate figure, nor was this possible in relation to the corporate recharge amounts. The added problem on the corporate recharge apportionment was the lack of explanation on the discounting factor and the integrity of it on the evidence. There was also a paucity of evidence, on the Tribunal's findings, as to how the charges were associated with the provision of services to the residents of Pelican Waters Village.

Operator Cannot Contract Out of Their Obligations

4.15 The Plaintiff has made much of the ground in their appeal that the Tribunal failed to recognise the contractual obligations imposed on residents for insurance, and by implication, the corporate recharge imposts. The provisions under s 199 of the Act have been consummately ignored by the Plaintiff. The irony is that under the very contractual obligations that the Plaintiff asserts they in fact incorporate the Act which they seek to avoid.

Signed Peter William Hill
Hill & Co Lawyers
For the Defendant
11th March 2011

Chapter 15

The District Court Hearing – Days 1 & 2

Jack and his wife Janice decided that as the Hearing was scheduled for two days they would travel to Sydney on the 10.00am XPT train from Wauchope on the 13th and stay two nights at the Great Southern Hotel in George Street, travelling back on the 4.10pm XPT from Central on Tuesday. If it was necessary because the case was going longer than expected they would change their travel arrangements and stay another night.

After breakfast at the hotel Jack and Janice caught a taxi up to 86 Goulburn Street, and after entering the building and going through security went to the 16th floor. The Hearing was scheduled to commence at 9.30am in court 16c and although it was not yet 9.00 Jack recognised several residents whom he had met a month earlier at the Directional Hearing held on the 8th February. By 9.30 there were 31 residents present including seven of the RVRA Committee. Peter Hill and his Para-Legal assistant Della Lane were also present as was Solicitor Arthur Kedis from Gladsons Lawyers and Ivan Gittoes a Barrister in wig and gown representing Landbuild.

The Hearing was listed for 9.30am before Ms Justice Rafter. The case was the first on the list and the Judge advised that the matter was to be heard before His Honour Judge L A Lewis SC, in Court 14c at 10.15am. All present then made their way down to level 14 and under direction from the Court Officer waited outside of the court as there was another matter in progress. Jack noticed that the name on the Court Officer's name tag was Bruce Wilkinson, a man in his early sixties of slight build with a neatly trimmed moustache and a dignified bearing, the type of fellow who would command respect and imparted an air of authority.

Just after 10.00am seven people left Court Room 14c and the Court Officer indicated to the assembled that they could enter the court room. The room was a little larger than the one used for the Directional Hearing one month earlier with the usual bench and high backed chair for the Judge and a smaller chair near the Judge's for his Associate. On the back wall behind the Judge's chair the New South Wales Coat of Arms was displayed. There was a witness box and in the centre of the room a long table with four chairs and at the centre of the table was a raised section or lectern where the legal representatives would stand and speak from. The room had a number of microphones located at various positions.

The supporting residents quickly occupied all of the thirty seats available, realising that more chairs were required the Court Officer went to another court room and brought in another six. Gittoes and Kedis, and Hill and Lane took their places at the long table with the Plaintiff's legal team on the left and the Defendants duo on the right. Jack took a seat behind Peter Hill and Pierce Burken and a fellow who Jack did not know, but presumed he was from Landbuild's legal branch took seats behind Gittoes and Kedis.

At 10.15am the Judge's Associate entered from a door behind the bench carrying various folders and took her seat. The Court Officer then came into the room from the same door and announced, "All stand". Judge Lewis entered the court room; Jack observed that he was a man in his mid-sixties, dressed in a grey business suit with a dark tie. When the Judge got to his seat he bowed to the legal table and all in the room replied with a bow. All then took their seats. The Associate then stated the case number and the names of the Plaintiff and Defendant.

Ivan Gittoes dressed in his wig and silk robe then stood and said, "Your Honour, my name is Ivan Gittoes, which is spelt, G-I-T-T-O-E-S, I appear on behalf of the Appellant, Pelican Waters Village Pty Ltd".

The Judge replied, "Thank you My Gittoes. I did not realise that we were dressing up this morning".

Gittoes stuttered, "I am sorry your Honour .... I just assumed .... with your permission Your Honour I will remove ....".

The Judge nodded, indicating that that is what he should do. Gittoes removed his wig and gown and handed them to Kedis sitting alongside him; Kedis took the apparel and shoved it under the table. Gittoes resumed his seat. Jack noticed that Gittoes who was a tall man in his fifties with a bald head now had a red tinge on his face having made a mistake in coming to the court over dressed. Jack could also feel that the audience were smiling to themselves and he thought to himself that they were off to a great start.

Peter Hill then rose and moved to the lectern, "Your Honour, my name is Peter Hill and I am representing the Defendants the Pelican Waters residents Association in this matter".

The Judge acknowledged Hill and Peter resumed his seat. Justice Lewis advised that he could allow one and a half days for the matter to proceed at this time. He then asked if the parties had prepared Submissions to present to the Court. Both Gittoes and Hill handed a copy of their Submission as had been exchanged between them last Friday to the Court Officer who took them to the Judge.

The Judge then said, "Mr Gittoes, do you wish to make an opening statement?"

Gittoes stood and moved to the lectern and placed and opened a folder and started to quote from it. Jack later learnt that the document he was referring to was the Plaintiff's Submission. It was apparent to everyone present that Gittoes had not done his homework, he rambled on and on filibustering and trying to summarise the Plaintiff's case. He was still going on at 12.50 when Judge Lewis advised that they would now break for lunch and resume at 2.00pm. The Court Officer on anticipating what was about to happen went to the front of the Court and announced, "All rise". All rose and bowed to the Judge who left the court room.

Jack and his wife Janice together with Malcom McKenzie and several of the RVRA Committee went to a local coffee shop where they discussed the morning's proceedings while they had lunch. Returning early they found Bruce Wilkinson the Court Officer present at the court room, he was a pleasant man who readily engaged in conversation with Jack and several others and said that he had been Court Officer for a number of Judge Lewis's cases and had always found him to be fair and one who would ask a lot of questions in order to get to the bottom of a matter, this gave Jack confidence that the Pelican Waters residents would get a fair go.

At 2.00pm the Court resumed with Gittoes continuing with his arguments as to why in his opinion the Orders issued by the CTTT Senior Member Mr Jones on the 8th November 2010 should be overturned. Ivan Gittoes went on arguing that Mr G. Jones had erred at law by not using his discretionary powers to find just what percentage or amount that the Residents should have been required to pay in respect to the two line items, Insurance and Corporate Recharge that were in dispute. He went to great length to quote various Sections and Clauses from the Retirement Village and CTTT legislation to try and prove his argument.

Jack had positioned himself in such so position that out of the corner of his eye he could see Pierce Burken and observed that there were a number of occasions when Burken would shake his head in disbelief of what Gittoes was saying. All the time that Gittoes was addressing the Judge he was receiving prompts from Arthur Kedis the instructing solicitor for Landbuild.

Judge Lewis questioned Ivan Gittoes on many of his references to the legislation and also questioned the relevance of some of his statements and how they were in support of his argument. There were several conversations between Justice Lewis and Mr Ivan Gittoes about the import and meaning of the words "May", Must" and "Shall".

When speaking about the insurance issue Gittoes quoted from the CTTT decision, *"In regard to insurance, the obligation is to pay the lessor's insurance premiums in respect of all buildings, fittings and fixtures against fire, flood, lightning, storm and tempest and in respect of insurance against all other risks referrable to Pelican Waters Village as the Council of Management may deem necessary or desirable".*

The Judge asked the question, "Do the residents have representation on the Council of Management?"

Without hesitation Gittoes said that they did. When Jack heard this he vigorously shook his head and scribbled a note for Peter Hill advising that although the contract mentioned a Council of Management there had never been one that involved residents' participation. Jack was sure that the Judge had picked up on his body language.

At 3.10pm Gittoes completed his opening statement much to the relief of all in attendance.

The Judge then invited Peter Hill to commence his opening statement. Peter Hill took only 20 minutes to present his opening submission which he did in a rehearsed and professional manner advancing the argument that it was not compulsory for Tribunal Member Jones to make a determination as to the percentage or amount that the Residents should contribute towards Insurance and Corporate Recharge, he also suggested that the Tribunal Member was unable to do so because of the lack of detail available to him in the operators submission.

Hill also raised the issue of a transcript of the Consumer Trader and Tenancy Tribunal; he advised that he had requested a copy from Gladsons Lawyers shortly after the Directional Hearing of the 8th February 2011 to be advised that a transcript was not available. On making his own enquiries he found out last Friday that a recording of the hearing was available. The Judge agreed that a transcript of what had been said at the Tribunal would be helpful and it was agreed that the Plaintiff would obtain a copy and a written transcript would be produced, this would take at least a week. Jack's memory went back to the CTTT Hearing when the Tribunal Member took a small recording device from his pocket and indicated to those present that the proceedings would be recorded.

At 3.30pm Peter Hill completed his opening submission and the Court was then adjourned till 10.30 the next morning.

The following day, Tuesday, 15th March 2011 Jack and Janice were up early and had breakfast at the Great Southern hotel after which they took their luggage up to the booking office at Central Station and booked it in for that afternoon's XPT train, Jack estimated that they would be away from the Court in time to catch the 4.12 train to the North Coast. Then they caught a taxi up to Goulburn Street arriving outside Court 14c just before 9.30am.

The only other people in the vicinity of the court room were Bruce Wilkinson the Court Officer and two Asian ladies whom Jack presumed were mother and daughter and were waiting outside of the court room which was opposite 14c. The two ladies were talking quietly between themselves when after about 10 minutes an Asian fellow arrived; he was carrying a two litre bottle of milk which he was drinking from. Jack thought to himself that it was a little unusual when the new arrival saw the two ladies and began in a loud voice to abuse them; there was definitely a conflict between the three.

When Bruce Wilkinson who had been in the court room heard the ruckus he came out and summing up the situation quietly went over to where Jack and Janice were sitting and suggested that they might be more comfortable in the court room, an invitation they readily accepted. Jack observed that as soon as he and his wife were in the court room the Court Officer used his mobile phone to call the buildings security who must have arrived fairly soon as the ruckus stopped just as quickly as it had started.

By 10.30am, the appointed time for the matter to be resumed there were 28 supporting residents, including six from the RVRA Executive and Committee seated to witness the day proceedings. Representing the operator were Ivan Gittoes, Barrister (not in wig and robe), Arthur Kedis, Solicitor and Pierce Burken. Representing the residents was Peter Hill with his assistant Della Lane.

Judge Lewis entered the Court with the usual formalities, he commenced by stating that he had read both submissions overnight. Gittoes was then given the opportunity to present argument as to why the CTTT decision should be overturned which he did for the next hour. Jack observed that Gittoes appeared to have a better knowledge of the matter before the Court today than he did yesterday and Jack thought to himself, "He must have spent most of the night familiarising himself with the case". Again the Judge interrupted him with questions and on occasion referred to Hill for his opinion or clarification on a certain point.

On one such occasion when the barrister for the operator said that the Tribunal Member should have made more effort to determine the residents proportion of the costs rather than remove the total. Judge Lewis pointed out that the Act said the CTTT member "may" but is not obliged to take more action. The judge pointed out that the premium advice was like scrambled eggs and it is not easy to unscramble eggs.

The Judge also asked the barrister hypothetically that if the CTTT member had determined an amount of 50% would the operators have accepted that and Gittoes said that he was unsure but thought that they would not have accepted an arbitrary split. The Judge then replied that in his opinion the CTTT member was probably better to delete the whole cost rather than guess on inadequate evidence provided.

At 11.30 Judge Lewis advised that the matter would be adjourned to enable him to hand down a decision in another matter. The Pelican Waters matter resumed at 12 Noon.

Peter Hill then had the opportunity to respond and occupied about 45 minutes in advancing his arguments in support of our defence of the CTTT decision. He presented copies of the 2000 Regulation, the Report to Parliament of 2005 and Hansard extracts from the time of the introduction of the Amendment Act in 2008.

Each time that Peter Hill got to his feet to speak Jack was impressed with his knowledge of the relevant legislation and the facts relating to the case. Jack was also impressed with the efficiency of Della Lane, Peter's assistant who was able to immediately put her hand to any section of legislation or paragraph contained in the CTTT evidence or other documents. Whereas the legal team for the operator seemed to be having trouble finding reference to whatever it was that Gittoes was referring to.

At 1.00pm the Judge adjourned the matter for a one hour lunch break. At exactly 2.00pm the Court resumed with the same persons present as prior to lunch.

For the next hour the Judge questioned both Gittoes and Hill on various point of interest. At about 3.00pm proceedings were interrupted by a very loud and heated argument outside the court room. Jack immediately recognised the voice of the Asian fellow who had caused a ruckus that morning, evidently the matter that he and the two Asian ladies had been involved in had been completed and not to his satisfaction.

The court room fell silent, even Gittoes who was in mid-sentence was speechless. Bruce Wilkinson the Court Officer hurried from the Court to ascertain what was happening and at the same time the Judge's Associate pressed a security alarm which was situated at her feet. This action summonsed several security officers who arrived in a very short time and subdued the Asian fellow who was placed in handcuffs and led away from level 14.

After things had settled down and Bruce Wilkinson had reported to the Judge that all was now in order and apologised to the Court for the interruption Judge Lewis suggested that the transcript of the CTTT Hearing should be considered before a decision was handed down. He decided that the matter be adjourned till the 8th April at 10.00am at which time both parties after considering the CTTT transcript would be allowed to make final submissions with the hope that a determination would be made on that day.

Jack and Peter thanked the members of the RVRA and village residents who had been there on the past two days in support of the Pelican Waters residents. Both Malcolm McKenzie and Jan Pritchett, the President and Secretary of the RVRA expressed the opinion that they thought Peter Hill had made a strong case on behalf of the residents and that they would be surprised if the matter was not found in favour of the residents. All then departed and went on their separate ways.

Jack and Janice were in time to catch their train and as they waited on Central Station Janice said to Jack, "I don't understand why Peter Hill and the other fellow kept referring to each other as '*My friend*' when it is very obvious that they don't like each other". Jack explained that Barristers refer to each other as '*My Learned Friend*' and refer to solicitors as '*My Friend*'. Therefore in the circumstances of their case where one of the legal representatives was a solicitor then the correct form of address between the two legal representatives was 'My friend".

Having arrived home safely, the following day Jack compiled a report which he placed in each Pelican Waters residents' letter box. The report summarised the events of the previous two days and also stated. *"I have found this a most interesting experience and am confident that the Residents of Pelican Waters Village will receive an outcome that will be just, and hopefully favourable to them. However, I am still concerned that the Residents of a village can be summonsed to defend an action that they were not responsible for; e.g. the decision of the CTTT in a Tribunal matter. I am of the opinion that in the case of CTTT decisions that are appealed to a higher authority, then the CTTT should be the Defendant or at least named as a joint Defendant in such matters. I look forward to the 8th April".*

Chapter 16

Waiting for the Decision

On Friday, 18th March the residents received the following from Landbuild:

Residents of Pelican Waters Village
Dear Residents,

Re: Update on District Court Hearing

We undertook to keep residents informed as to the progress of the above hearing and therefore provide the following by way of an update.

The hearing took place over 2 days on 14 and 15 March 2011 with both parties, Peter Hill for the Pelican Waters residents and Ivan Gittoes for Landbuild, putting forward their respective cases.

Judge L A Lewis SC then advised that he required more time to review the material provided and consider the CTTT transcripts before handing down his decision.

The hearing is set to reconvene on 8 April 2011 at which time both parties will be asked to make their final submissions. At this time Judge Lewis will provide a decision which will provide clarity around a number of matters for all parties.

We thank you for your patience and will keep you updated as the matter progresses.

In the meantime, if you have any further queries or concerns, please do not hesitate to contact us.

Yours sincerely

Alice Watson
General Manager, Operations - Retirement Living

When Jack received the letter he thought that this manner of communication was completely different to the approach previously taken by Dollarvill, who seemed to have the policy of not responding to correspondence of any kind and of keeping residents in the dark. Jack also reflected that maybe the situation might have been different if Pierce Burken had not been involved in the 2010-11 budget negotiations and he was fairly sure that if Burken had not been appointed as NSW Operations Manager after the take-over by Landbuild then perhaps the CTTT decision would not have been appealed to the District Court.

During the next two weeks Jack, Bob and Shirley meet several times to formulate information following requests from Peter Hill, there were numerous phone calls and emails. On Friday, 1st April Peter Hill received a copy of the transcript of the CTTT Hearing a copy of which he promptly sent to Jack. Over the weekend Jack studied the transcript and on Monday, 4th April Jack and Peter had a long phone conversation and the more they analyzed the transcript the more confident they became of a favourable outcome.

Evidently the operator's legal team had also been busy over the weekend which resulted in Jack receiving from Peter Hill a copy of a letter he had received by email that morning:

By Email to Hill & Company Lawyers.
Dear Peter,

Pelican Waters Village Pty Ltd v Pelican Waters Village Residents Association

District Court of NSW at Sydney, Proceeding No: 2010/999999

We refer to our telephone conversation on 4 April 2011.

As your clients will recall, prior to the commencement of these proceedings in the District Court, our client wrote directly to Mr Clarke and others on 3 February 2011, to notify them of the pending application and the basis for bringing the action. As stated in those letters, our client indicated it accepted the comments made by the Consumer Trader & Tenancy Tribunal (CTTT) as to the need to provide greater transparency on budget matters but did not consider the CTTT was correct in completely removing the two items of expenditure given the purpose and effect of the Retirement Villages Act 1999 (NSW) (the Act) and the village contracts. As our client said, its objective has been to obtain clarity on the issues and the budgetary process.

As you are also aware, our client operates another village called Junebrook Manor Retirement Village at which similar issues as raised in these proceedings were also the subject of other CTTT proceedings. As you are aware, our client was the Applicant in other CTTT proceedings namely Junebrook Manor Pty Ltd v The Residents of Junebrook Manor Retirement Village. This matter was heard in December 2010 and March 2011. You acted for the residents at the hearing on 16 March 2011.

The CTTT handed down its decision in the Junebrook matter on 16 March 2011. That decision addressed the CTTT proceedings in this matter and provided further clarity on the budgetary process and operation of the Act.

Since the hearing of the CTTT proceedings, our client has moved to provide the greater transparency referred to in this matter and Maybrook and has been engaged with its residents in the budgetary processes for the year ended 30 June 2012. We are instructed that the process and level of transparency adopted has been well received by the residents.

In all of the circumstances, our client is of the view that the object of providing clarity to the parties and the operation of the Act in relation to the budgetary process has been achieved by operation of these CTTT proceedings and the decision in Junebrook.

For all of these reasons, our client sees no further utility in maintaining these proceedings and seeks to discontinue these proceedings. In seeking such discontinuance, we see no prejudice to your clients for at least the following reasons:

1. the Plaintiff commenced the proceedings to seek clarity as to budgetary process and matters of law, which clarity our client says has been provided by the principles in this matter and the Junebrook CTTT determination;

2. the Plaintiff does not want the Defendants to be compelled to continue litigation;

3. the Plaintiff has agreed to pay all of the Defendant's costs of the litigation up to a maximum of $50,000 plus GST; and

4. For all these reasons, the Defendant will not be prejudiced by the discontinuance of the proceedings. On the contrary, the effect of the discontinuance will be to leave the CTTT's orders intact.

In order to save further time and costs, please confirm whether your client, Pelican   Waters Village Residents Association ,will consent to discontinuance of the proceedings by signing the enclosed notice of discontinuance and return to us for filing by no later than 5pm on 6 April 2011.

We note from our conversation, you anticipate such a request will be rejected.

We confirm we are instructed to file a notice of motion to seek the leave of the court to discontinue the proceedings pursuant to rule 12.1(l)(b) of the Uniform Civil Procedure Rules 2005 (NSW). We will seek for this motion to be listed on 8 April 2011. If your clients consent to the discontinuance of the proceedings, we can provide the enclosed consent to the Court in place of the motion. If your clients do not consent to the discontinuance, the motion will be heard. Our client reserves the right to seek orders dismissing the appeal with costs.

We put you on notice that we will rely upon this letter and previous correspondence between the parties in support of that application.

Yours sincerely

  Arthur Kedis

  Gladsons Lawyers

The above letter stated that Landbuild now wanted to withdraw their appeal; however, both Jack and Peter were concerned about the statement, "*Our client reserves the right to seek orders dismissing the appeal with costs*". This they regarded as a stand over tactic, a threat implying, "*do as we want or it could cost your client a lot of money*". This veiled threat was typical of Dollarvill's attitude which had been confirmed by the actions of appealing the CTTT decision to the District Court. It had been stated by Pierce Burken, *"We will take you, (the residents) to the Tribunal and if we don't win there we will appeal it to the District or Supreme Court, and you had better have deep pockets"*.

As Burken was still the New South Wales Operations Manager Jack reckoned that he was the one giving instructions to Landbuild's legal team and in doing so was trying to not only save a little face over what was developing into a losing situation for Landbuild, but a situation that might put his position with the company in jeopardy.

Peter Hill sent an email to Arthur Kedis in which he asked, *"Could you urgently confirm that you are now indicating that should our client be unsuccessful in their opposition to your petition for discontinuance, then you reserve the right to withdraw your client's earlier undertaking concerning the payment of our client's costs up to an amount of $50,000 plus GST. We look forward to hearing from you on this in writing as a matter of urgency"*.

A short time later Peter Hill received the following email from Arthur Kedis:

Dear Mr Hill

Thank you for your email.

You have misinterpreted our letter and our client's reservation. Our client is reserving the right to make application to have the proceedings dismissed.

Irrespective of whether the application for discontinuance is successful or not, our client is not withdrawing or in any way disturbing its undertaking to meet payment of your client's costs of the Appeal proceedings up to an amount of $50,000 plus GST.

My apologies if the language of our correspondence has caused some confusion.

It appeared that there had been a change of mind and that the offer to meet the residents' costs up to $50,000 plus GST was still on the table. This was confirmed with a copy of a *"Notice of Motion"* which had been filed in the District Court seeking orders:

1. *"that pursuant to rule 12.1(1)(b) of the Uniform Procedures Rules 2005 (NSW) the Applicant is granted leave to discontinue the Summons to appeal made by the Applicant in these proceedings.*
2. *The Applicant to pay the Respondent's costs of the action on an indemnity basis.*
3. *Such further or other orders as the Court sees fit.*

The Notice had been lodged by Landbuild's legal representative, Arthur Kedis.

Just before lunch on the day that the above communications were going on Jack received a phone call from Alice Watson who advised that she was the newly appointed General Manager, Operations for Landbuild Retirement Living. She explained that Landbuild were concerned about the stress being placed upon the Pelican Waters residents and the time and expense that the District Court matter was taking up and that the management team had decided to withdraw the application and comply with the decision of the CTTT. It was also expressed that she hoped that the residents and Landbuild management team could now put all of this business behind them and move forward in a partnership that would benefit all concerned.

Jack advised that he could not make such a decision; however, he would attempt to call a meeting of the available members of the Residents Committee together that afternoon and if there was a quorum present they would discuss the matter and he would phone her back as soon as possible.

After phoning around Jack was able to get, as well as himself, six members of the committee to agree to meet at 2.00pm that day. During the hastily convened committee meeting Jack reported on the happenings of that day as well as his opinion of what the transcript of the CTTT Hearing showed. After an hour of discussion during which Bob McTavish stated that *"there is a need for 'principles to proceed' as the matter needs to be permanently settled"*, it was unanimously resolved that the matter should continue to be determined by the District Court, therefore the offer of Landbuild that the application be withdrawn be not accepted.

Jack immediately phoned Peter Hill and advised him of the Committee's decision. He then phoned Alice Watson and told her of the decision that the Committee had arrived at and explained that the main reason was that whenever the residents had sought a compromise to end the matter they were told that the matter needed to be resolved one way or the other. The residents were now adamant that the matter should proceed to its end in order that some of the lack of clarity in the retirement village legislation might be made clearer.

Anticipating that the Landbuild legal team would present arguments on Friday in support of having the matter withdrawn from the District Court three affidavits were prepared with the assistance of Peter Hill. These were from Jack Clarke, Bob McTavish and Shirley Dunlop. Some of the points raised in the affidavits were:

1. *I have read the notice of motion filed in these proceedings by the Plaintiff including the supporting affidavit of Mr Kedis. I have also read a copy of the transcript of the proceedings on the last day of the hearing in the case of Junebrook Manor Pty Ltd v The Residents of Maybrook Manor Retirement Village (the Junebrook Manor Case) heard in the CTTT on 16 March 2011 which contained an oral judgement by Tribunal Member Jones. This case dealt with identical issues relating to insurance costs and corporate recharge items as those that exist in the current proceedings and included the same*

operator as the Plaintiff in these proceedings. I am also aware that evidence that was provided on affidavit in those proceedings from a Mr Burken and Mr Lam was the same or of similar import to that provided by those witnesses in the Pelican Waters CTTT dispute.

2. *The decision of Mr Martin in the Junebrook Manor Case is of opposite effect to that of Tribunal Member Jones in the Pelican Waters case. This creates enormous uncertainty for residents at Pelican Waters Village in relation to the principles that apply, and if not resolved, will in my view only add to the disputation in the future at our village in relation to these issues. I verily believe that should the Plaintiffs motion in these proceedings be successful, the defendant will be denied an opportunity to potentially have some clarity and legal certainty in relation to the matters currently before the Court. The Plaintiff in these proceedings had earlier agreed to cover residents' costs arising from these proceedings. If this had not occurred, we would not have been represented at this hearing. This was largely in recognition of the disadvantaged position the residents are in not having the funds to either defend proceedings or take them in their own right in relation to important matters of principle. This will continue in to the future. The matters before the Court do constitute important matters of principle and the opportunity now before the Court to finally determine these issues and hand down a decision one*

way or the other will be lost if the current proceedings are discontinued.

3. The Pelican Waters Residents Association comprises elderly persons, many of whom suffer quite serious health issues and find it difficult at the particular time in their life to carry the baton on important issues, unlike the operator who has largely unlimited funds and resources to prosecute its position to its benefit. It is at times hard going and exhausting which is not only a product of our age and health concerns but also our lack of technical expertise.

4. Study has shown that Tribunal decisions on the same subject matter are from time to time at variance with one another. This does create immense challenges for residents.

5. Since the decision by the CTTT in the Pelican Waters case, the operator of our village has been taken over by the Landbuild Group. It is a fact that in the past 3 years a significant process of amalgamation has occurred across the retirement village industry in NSW and beyond. With the onset of this development, has come the onset of corporate recharge costs being required to be paid, which at our village, prior to the Dollarvill takeover, were not a feature of our budgetary process.

6. I am aware across NSW that there are numerous other villages where residents are in dispute with the operator over issues which include those now being agitated before the District

Court. These include the following villages in NSW; Minkara Retirement Village, Bayview Gardens Retirement Village, Maple Grove Retirement Village, Alloura Waters Retirement Village, The Landings Retirement Village, Mountain View Murwillumbah retirement Village, Mountain View Retirement Village, Leura Fairways Retirement Village and Carey Bay Retirement Village. A number of these villages either have CTTT proceedings in progress or are awaiting CTTT decisions.

7. *I believe it would not only disadvantage the residents of Pelican Waters Village for the current proceedings to be discontinued and thereby deny them an opportunity one way or the other for some principles in relation to these matters to be decided, but would not serve the administration of justice across the retirement village industry in NSW.*

8. *In future disputes with the Plaintiff that involves these issues, the Association does not have the financial resources to take any adverse ruling in the CTTT to a higher Court and the opportunity allowed by these current proceedings to clarify the position will therefore be denied.*

9. *It is apparent that in the Resident Association's current discussions with the operator in relation to items of insurance and corporate recharge costs for the 2010/2011 budget for the village, they continue to hold to the view that they expect residents to pay for insurance costs beyond those matters allowed by Tribunal Member Jones in the Pelican Waters*

CTTT decision and have kept with their method of calculation relied on in that case in respect to corporate recharge items. The issues of transparency and information provided by the operator, continues to be a real problem for the Committee.

10. In the notice of motion of the Plaintiff dated 4 April 2011 before the District Court in these proceedings at annexure 'A' to the supporting affidavit of Mr Kedis is a letter from Landbuilds CEO Henry Wilson to myself. At paragraph five of the letter Mr Wilson states Landbuilds belief that the CTTT decision that is the subject of these proceedings 'does not provide clarity for residents or operators about how charges should be handled in the future'. At paragraph six of the letter Mr Wilson indicates that Landbuilds position is that this matter requires 'clarification of the law to protect the best interests of all parties'. I agree with this position. It is my firm belief that the contrary decision passed down by the CTTT in the Junebrook Manor Case increases the need for this clarification rather than reducing it as the plaintiff now claims. In my view the contrary decision handed down by the CTTT in the Junebrook Manor case highlights the fact that the law that governs the issues of insurance and corporate recharge items needs clarification so that all parties are well informed of their rights and obligations so as to make informed decisions when these issues arise in relation to budgetary discussions in the future. I certainly believe that in the event this matter does not follow through to completion

residents of Pelican Waters Village and likely residents of other villages within the Landbuild portfolio will suffer the great disadvantage of being denied the benefit of clarification that this Court is in a position to provide surrounding a contentious issue that will without doubt reoccur in the future.

The three affidavits were duly signed and witnessed that day by a JP who under Peter Hill's direction was not a resident of Pelican Waters Village. The affidavits were then packaged and Jack delivered them to a courier company at the Port Macquarie airport in order that Hill and Company would receive them the next morning. They were then forwarded to the District Court in time for Judge Lewis to consider their content prior to the Hearing resuming on the 8th April.

Chapter 17

The District Court Hearing and Decision – Day 3

The morning of Friday, 8th April arrived; again Jack was up early in order to be at Port Macquarie airport in time to take the 6.30am flight to Sydney. On arrival in Sydney Jack had time for breakfast before making his way up to Goulburn Street. He checked the lists for that day's proceedings which detailed court rooms allocated to the various matters to be heard that day. The Pelican Waters matter was again listed in Court 14c.

When Jack arrived in the corridor outside Court 14c at 9.25am he found that the only other person there was Bruce Wilkinson, the Court Officer who Jack had spoken to on previous occasions. Jack greeted Bruce with an outstretched hand which was readily accepted and the two men shook hands as two old friends would have. They conversed for about fifteen minutes without mentioning the Pelican Waters case as Jack considered that it would not have been appropriate for Bruce to do so. However, Bruce did say that he had always found Judge Lewis to be very fair in his judgments and a fellow who took his responsibilities very seriously and always did his 'homework'.

At about 9.40 Malcolm McKenzie and Jan Pritchett arrived as did Peter Hill and his assistant Della Lane. The five stood talking for a short time with Peter expressing the belief that he was sure that the three affidavits would carry the day as far as the Motion to discontinue the matter was concerned. Every couple of minutes the lift doors would open and village residents who Jack recognised as being at the previous Hearing days entered the corridor near Court 14c. Jack observed that there were again about 30 supporters present. At 9.55am those present went into the court room and took their seats.

Ivan Gittoes and Arthur Kedis were in their places at the table as were Peter and Della, Jack as previously took the seat nearest to Peter Hill and at 10.00am the Court was resumed with the usual formalities. Jack noticed that Pierce Burken was not present.

Judge Lewis commenced by stating that he had read the transcript of the CTTT Hearing and also the affidavits that had been tendered to the Court yesterday. Gittoes was requested to give his closing statement. He commenced by stating that the Motion to discontinue was being withdrawn because the Defendant wished the matter to be decided by the Court. Gittoes then continued by repeating some of his previous arguments as to why Senior Tribunal Member Mr Jones had erred in not apportioning the residents liability for their proportion of insurance and corporate recharge. This took about forty minutes.

Hill was then given the opportunity to present his closing statement which he did by summarizing the facts pertaining to the residents' case in a brief and capable manner.

Judge Lewis advised that he would consider this morning's statements together with the evidence previously conveyed to the Court. As he had another matter to deal with at 11.30am he adjourned the matter advising that he would hand down his judgement at 3.45pm this day.

Jack, Malcolm, Jan and a couple of others had a leisurely lunch together at a convenient café whilst discussing the events leading up to and including this morning. All who had been present in the morning were again present prior to 3.45pm. At the appointed hour Judge Lewis entered the Court and proceeded without hesitation to deliver his judgment.

1. He quoted the case number, the name of the Plaintiff and Respondent then said, "I make the following orders":

> "(1) The appeal by Pelican Waters Village Pty Ltd is dismissed;
>
> (2) The orders made on 9 December 2010 by the Consumer, Trader and Tenancy Tribunal in proceedings before it numbered RV 10/28914 and RV 10/31794 are confirmed;
>
> (3) Pelican Waters Village Pty Ltd is to pay the costs of the Pelican Waters Village Residents Association on the ordinary basis unless otherwise ordered;
>
> (4) The exhibits may be returned;
>
> (5) Liberty to apply on 7 days' notice if further orders are required."

"Thank you Mr Gittoes, thank you Mr Hill". With that the Judge handed two copies of his judgement to Bruce Wilkinson who passed one to Ivan Gittoes and one to Peter Hill, the Judge then got up from his chair and left the court room.

Jack was astounded not only that the judgement was totally in favour of the residents, but that the hundreds of hours spent in compiling the evidence, the affidavits, the phone calls and emails had all been reduced to five points delivered by the Judge in less than a minute.

When the Judge and his Associate had left the Court Jack went to Peter Hill, the two men shook hands and Jack thanked Peter for all of his efforts on behalf of the Pelican Waters residents. Peter responded with, "No Jack it is you and your team who have to be thanked and also the Pelican Waters residents for having the courage to accept the challenge that had been placed before them and without hesitation to run the case. The precedent that has been set here today will give all retirement village residents in this State the right to transparency in their budgets".

After receiving congratulations from the RVRA Executive and many of the village residents who had come from many different villages Jack found a quiet corner and phoned Janice and told her of the good news. Although Jack's wife had not been actively involved in hours put into the defence of the matter, she had been there to allow her home to be used for the holding of many meetings, and to give moral support to her husband's endeavours. Jack asked Janice to let Michael Austin know the result in order that he might tell the fellows at 'Secret Men's Business' that afternoon as he would not be home till about 7.00pm.

Jack then phoned Shirley and briefly told her what had transpired and requested that she let Bob and whoever else she came across know the result. She assured that it would be her pleasure to do so.

When Jack arrived home he sent the following email to each person who he had an email address for who had in some way expressed support for the Pelican Waters residents.

> *Hi All,*
>
> *The Pelican Waters Village District Court matter was finalised today.*
>
> *The Judge Ordered that the operators Application to have the CTTT Decision of 9th December which was favourable to the Residents, DISMISSED.*
>
> *The Judge then Ordered that the CTTT Decision that the two line items in the 2010-11 budget, namely Insurance $23,100 and Corporate Recharge (Managements Fees) $28,594 be removed. Thus saving the Residents $51,694 this year.0*
>
> *Costs were also awarded against the operator.*
>
> *I will not know if there are to be any on flowing benefits for the Residents in this village and possibly Residents in villages throughout the State until I receive the Judge's written findings.*
>
> *There were about 30 Residents from other villages present in court today including five members of the RVRA Committee*

supporting the Pelican waters residents cause and I extend my
thanks to each of them.

Regards,
Jack Clarke

As Jack had had to drive from the Port Macquarie airport to home a trip of about thirty minutes he did not allow himself the pleasure of a celebratory drink until he arrived home and after greeting his wife he sent the above email then poured himself a large scotch and said to himself, "Bloody hell Mate, that was tough, I don't think I would want to go through all of that again, here's to Pelican Waters".

Chapter 18

The Judge's Written Judgement

The following day Jack received a copy of the Judge's written Judgement by email from Peter Hill. After reading through the 26 pages Jack reckoned that the document was not produced between the time that the Judge dealt with his 11.30am matter and 2.00pm when he handed down his Judgement. Jack surmised that it had been developed prior to the 8th.

The written Judgement is as follows:

Pelican Waters Village Pty Ltd v Pelican Waters Village Residents Association

[2011] NSW DC 21 (8 April 2011)

District Court New South Wales

Case Title: Pelican Waters Village Pty Ltd v
                 Pelican Waters Village Residents Association

Hearing Date(s): 14 & 15 March, 8 April 2011

Decision Date: 08 April 2011

Jurisdiction: Civil

Before: Lewis SC DCJ

Decision: 1.The appeal by Pelican Waters Village Pty Ltd is dismissed;

2.The orders made on 9 December 2010 by the Consumer, Trader and Tenancy Tribunal in proceedings numbered RV 10/999999 and RV 10/999998 are confirmed;

3.Pelican Waters Village Pty Ltd is to pay the costs of the Pelican Waters Village Residents Association on the ordinary basis unless otherwise ordered;

4.The exhibits may be returned;

5.Liberty to apply on 7 days notice if further orders are required.

[Note: The Uniform Civil Procedure Rules 2005 provide (Rule 36.11) that unless the Court otherwise orders, a judgment or order is taken to be entered when it is recorded in the Court's computerised court record system. Setting aside and variation of judgments or orders is dealt with by Rules 36.15, 36.16, 36.17 and 36.18. Parties should in particular note the time limit of fourteen days in Rule 36.16.]

Catchwords: ADMINISTRATIVE LAW - appeal from decision of Consumer Trader and Tenancy Tribunal - whether questions have arisen pursuant to s 67(1) of the Consumer Trader and Tenancy Tribunal Act 2001 with respect to matters of law - whether evidence mandated that CTTT exercise statutory discretion in favour of appellant; INTERPRETATION OF STATUTES - whether purposive construction of applicable provisions of the Retirement Villages Act 2009 and the applicable regulations under the Retirement Villages Regulation 2009 permits the operator of a retirement village to impose on the residents certain overhead items of contentious expenditure - whether refusal of CTTT to so order involves a question with respect to a matter of law

Legislation Cited: Consumer Trader and Tenancy Tribunal Act 2001,s67(1)
Retirement Villages Act 1999, ss 100, 107, 108, 112,115,199

Retirement Villages Regulation 2009, reg 17,

reg 26.

Uniform Civil Procedure Rules 2005, r 12.1(b)

Cases Cited: Antaios Compannia Naviera SA v Salen
Rederierna AB [1985] AC 191

House v The King [1936] HCA 40; (1936) 55
CLR 499

Toll (FGCT) Pty Ltd v Alphapharm Pty Ltd
[2004] HCA 52; 219 CLR 165

Texts Cited: Hansard, Retirement Villages Bill 1999, Second
Reading

Category: Principal judgment

Parties: Pelican Waters Village Pty Ltd (Appellant)

Pelican Waters Village Residents Association
(Respondent)

Representation

- Counsel: Mr I Gittoes (Appellant)

Mr PW Hill, solicitor (Respondent)

- Solicitors: Gladsons (Appellant)

Hill & Co (Respondent)

File number(s):   2010/999999

Publication
Restriction:

Judgment Table of Contents

Summons	[1]
Nature of dispute and parties	[2] - [4]
Factual background	[5] - [10]
Findings made by the Tribunal	[11] - [14]
Procedural matters	[15] - [23]
Transcript of the proceedings before CTTT	[24] - [34]
Grounds of Appeal	[35] - [36]
Contentions of the parties	[37] - [39]
Argued errors concerning questions with respect to matters of law	[40] - [42]
Relief sought by appellant	[43] - [44]
Issues central to the outcome of the appeal	[45] - [46]
Evidence before the CTTT and in the appeal	[47] - [48]

Summons

1. This summons involves an appeal pursuant to s 67(1) of the *Consumer Trader and Tenancy Tribunal Act* 2001 ["*CTTT Act*"]. The appeal is from a decision of the Retirement Villages Division of the Consumer, Trader and Tenancy Tribunal ["CTTT"]. Those proceedings were heard by Senior Member

285

G Jones at Port Macquarie on 8 November 2010. The decision of the CTTT was made on 9 December 2010.

Nature of dispute and parties

2. The appellant, Pelican Waters Village Pty Ltd ["the operator"] is the owner of a retirement village situated at 349 Ocean Drive Laurieton, NSW [" the retirement village "]. The respondent, Pelican Waters Village Residents Association is the residents' association whose members have a relevant interest in the operation of that retirement village [" the residents "].

3. The operator and the residents have found themselves in dispute as to certain insurance expenses and certain business overhead costs. The operator has indicated that it proposed to require the residents to bear those disputed costs. The parties took their dispute to the CTTT for adjudication. In the CTTT the dispute was determined in favour of the residents. The operator is dissatisfied with the decision of the CTTT, and claims the decision involved errors concerning questions with respect to matters of law.

4. The determination of the matters in dispute in this appeal necessarily involves a consideration of the basis for decision of the CTTT, the contractual relationship of the parties, principles of statutory interpretation and a consideration of whether the CTTT truly failed to exercise discretions conferred upon it by

statute, as is claimed by the operator, so as to amount to errors concerning questions with respect to matters of law.

Factual Background

5. The operator is owned by a publicly listed company, Dollarvill Ltd ["Dollarvill"] which, operates 30 retirement villages and 367 other facilities comprising nursing homes, aged care facilities and low care hostel facilities. For the purposes of operating those businesses, Dollarvill employs 582 employees in its group of business entities. In addition to operating its businesses at various individual locations, such as at the retirement village in question at Laurieton, for understandable reasons of practicality and business efficiency, a number of business activities and functions of Dollarvill are conducted from Dollarvill's central head office location. There is no dispute that in respect of its trading and business operations, Dollarvill, as the operator of those businesses, incurs significant annual expenses in connection with the running of those businesses at all of its various locations.

6. The *Retirement Villages Act* 1999 [" *RV Act* "] and the *Retirement Villages Regulation* 2009 [" *RV Regulations* "] provide rights, mechanisms and procedures for an operator to prepare an annual budget of anticipated expenses for the residents of a retirement village to approve for a forthcoming financial year. The mechanism provides for a budget to be placed before a management committee of residents of a

retirement village for approval in anticipation of the expenses being levied against the residents in the forthcoming year. The budget in question in the CTTT proceedings, which is the subject of this appeal, was presented to the residents in accordance with those prescribed procedures. The residents raised objections to several items in the budget. The residents are not the owners of any property in the retirement village, they are simply lessees. However, they have rights as consumers. Those rights arise as a matter of contractual relationship and by statute.

7. The contractual basis of the operator's entitlement to seek the payment of overheads is found in the definition of " *outgoings* " in the contracts between the operator and the residents. Outgoings are relevantly identified as follows:

" *'Outgoings'* means (to the extent to which the same are not specifically payable from time to time by any Lessee of any part of Pelican Waters Village) the total cost of all outgoings costs and expenses of the Lessor now or hereafter <u>properly and reasonably assessed charged or chargeable</u> paid or payable or otherwise incurred upon or <u>in respect of the whole of Pelican Waters Village and the Village Centre or</u> upon the Lessor in relation thereto <u>or in the conduct management and maintenance of Pelican Waters Village</u> and the use and occupation of the same as a high-class retirement village and the Village Centre as a high-class administrative and communal centre.

Fees payable by the Lessor to its auditors or to the Trustee shall not be included in general outgoings." [*Emphasis added*]

8. The matter at issue in the CTTT was the permissibility of the operator including in its annual budget for payment by the residents, two items of likely expenditure for the village in the forthcoming year. Those items comprised certain insurance costs, and some amounts for administrative and business overhead expenses, described as corporate recharge expenses, likely to be incurred by the operator in the forthcoming year.

9. The residents did not dispute the statutory entitlement of the operator to make levies of the kind sought. However, the residents disputed the proper identification of the amounts sought to be paid and the transparency of the particular amounts as sought by the operator. The residents disputed the characterisation of those amounts as being legitimately and properly passed on to them as being amounts reasonably assessed or chargeable in respect of the Pelican Waters Village. The basis of the dispute arose from the definition of outgoings in the contract between the parties, according to the elements of the definition to which I have added emphasis. The amounts in question were $23,100 in respect of insurance, and $28,954 in respect of a broad category of items described as corporate recharge expenses.

10. In the CTTT, that dispute was resolved in favour of the residents. The operator was dissatisfied with that decision and

has therefore appealed as of right to this court, pursuant to s 67(1) of the *CTTT Act* , claiming the decision of the CTTT was afflicted with errors concerning questions with respect to matters of law.

Findings made by the CTTT

11. The formal finding and order made by the CTTT was as follows:

    "2. Pursuant to the provisions of the *Retirement Villages Act 1999*, s 115(2)(e) an order is made that the line item of " *insurance* " in the sum of $23,100.00 and the line item of " *corporate recharge* " in the sum of $28,594.00 are both excluded from the budget for Pelican Waters Retirement Village for the financial year 2010-2011."

12. The CTTT gave detailed, transparently clear, cogent and logically structured reasons for its decision, in a series of 77 numbered paragraphs. Those reasons make it plain that before arriving at the findings on the matters in dispute, the CTTT Senior Member canvassed relevant matters. Those included the detail and the basis of the operator's application, the procedural course taken during the hearing, the issue of jurisdiction, and an appropriate review of the respective submissions of the parties. In making his findings, the CTTT Senior Member set out the relevant provisions of ss 100, 106-108 and 115 of the

RV Act , as well as the provisions of regulation 26 of the *RV Regulations* .

13. In reaching that reasoned determination, which is now challenged by the operator as being vitiated by contended errors concerning questions with respect to matters of law, the CTTT Senior Member identified certain categories of expenditure that by law, must not be financed by way of recurrent charges to be passed on to the residents.

14. On appeal, the operator submitted that in arriving at his determination, the CTTT Senior Member had failed to exercise relevant statutory discretions that were provided for under the cited legislation.

Procedural matters

15. The transcript of the proceedings before the CTTT was not available at the commencement of the hearing of this appeal. Notwithstanding that position, the parties took what I considered to be an unusual course by proceeding with the appeal without the transcript of the CTTT hearing. In conformity with that decision, the appeal proceeded to the stage of concluding the evidence and the delivery of final submissions. This was because the parties had agreed that since the subject matter of the appeal principally concerned construction of the relevant legislative provisions, they had agreed that the appeal could conveniently proceed on the basis

of an examination of the orders made by the CTTT, together with the underlying documentary evidence that was before the CTTT. In that regard, they considered that they could do without the transcript of the proceedings in the CTTT. The initial hearing of the appeal took place in this court on that basis on 14 and 15 March 2011.

16. During the course of final submissions, on 15 March 2011, the parties changed course and decided that after all, it would be prudent to defer finalising their arguments and submissions in order to obtain the transcript of the CTTT proceedings. That course was taken because it became apparent that the outcome of the appeal may turn on the issue of whether the CTTT had before it by way of submissions on behalf of the operator, a request that it exercise the statutory discretions that were now contended on appeal, and whether the evidence justified that course. The proceedings were then adjourned to 8 April 2011 for that purpose in order to conclude the arguments after a consideration of that transcript.

17. On 5 April 2011, my Associate was provided with a copy of the transcript of the CTTT proceedings in anticipation of the resumed hearing today. On 6 April 2011 the solicitors for the operator provided my Associate with a copy of a Notice of Motion filed on 4 April 2011, in which the operator sought to discontinue the appeal. That motion was supported by the affidavit of the solicitor for the operator, Mr Arthur Kedis,

sworn 4 April 2011. By that motion, the operator sought leave to discontinue its appeal, pursuant to r 12.1(b) of the Uniform Civil Procedures Rules 2005. In its motion, the operator indicated its consent to an order that it pay the costs of the residents on an indemnity basis on such a discontinuance.

18. At the commencement of the hearing of the appeal on 14 March 2011, I was informed that this appeal was considered by the parties to be a test case, by which the operator sought to clarify certain matters of law with respect to its proposed charges.

19. Paragraph 21 of Mr Kedis' affidavit is in the following terms:

"On 16 February 2010, we were informed by the CTTT that no transcript or sound recording existed in relation to the Tribunal Proceedings."

20. It appears that the reference to the 16 February 2010 date of the advice from the CTTT to the effect that there was no transcript or sound recording of the proceedings should clearly have been a reference to 16 February 2011. It was clearly apparent that when these proceedings were commenced, no transcript of the CTTT proceedings was available. However, it is now apparent that when that transcript was obtained on 28 March 2011, on instructions from the operator, the solicitors for the operator sought to discontinue the appeal.

21. Today, when the motion filed on 4 April 2011 was called on for hearing, it was withdrawn and the parties agreed that the applicant/plaintiff should pay the respondent/ defendant's costs on the ordinary basis. I made orders in those terms, and the remainder of the appeal then proceeded to conclusion.

22. It was also plain from the affidavits filed by the residents in connection with the dismissed motion, that they wanted an adjudication on the matters raised by the operator in this appeal in order to settle as soon as practicable, the claimed questions with respect to matters of law.

23. In the course of final arguments, I was referred to an interim transcript of reasons determining other proceedings in the CTTT between the operator in this case, and the residents of another of its retirement villages, in which similar issues were litigated. The transcript of reasons in the other matter was not full or final, and I took the view that whilst it could be argued to be persuasive, it was not determinative of the present appeal with which I am concerned. Accordingly, I then heard the remaining arguments to conclusion, in order to give this final judgment on the appeal.

Transcript of the proceedings before the CTTT

24. Today, on the resumed hearing of the appeal, the transcript of the CTTT proceedings, which comprised 33 pages, was

formally tendered: Exhibit "B". I had already had the opportunity of reading it when the parties had forwarded it for that purpose on 5 April 2011. Today I heard submissions based on that transcript, which shows that in the CTTT hearing, one of the residents, Mr Clarke, appeared as a representative spokesman of the residents. The operator was represented by its employee, Mr Burken. Neither were legal practitioners.

25. An examination of the transcript of the interchanges that took place between the CTTT Senior Member and the representatives of the parties reveals that the parties had been provided with an adequate opportunity to present relevant evidence and arguments in order to advance their respective positions. It clearly emerges from the transcript that the CTTT Senior Member had pointed out to the operator that the residents were concerned at the arbitrary, "*fictitious*" or non-factual basis upon which the operator had assigned and raised the claimed expenses for insurance and corporate recharge expenses.

26. This was in the context of evidence that the operator was involved in the running of a number of different but similar facilities, which incurred common or shared expenses, and where the operator sought to rely upon a percentage method of dividing or assigning those costs to this particular retirement village.

27. The nub of the objections raised by the residents concerned the operator's request that they pay for such artificially calculated sums. It was claimed it was not transparently apparent from the evidence, that the amounts sought by the operator were factually and temporally related to the particular retirement village in question. It was also argued that such expenses were not restricted only to categories of expense that the legislation permitted to be passed on to the residents. The concern of the residents, as consumers, was to ensure that only properly raised charges should be the subject of such a request for payment by them.

28. In the CTTT, the residents made reference to their concern that they should only be required to pay expenses that were permitted by the legislation. In that regard they pointed to claimed insurance costs not being restricted to the specific matters permitted or authorised by statute, namely reinstatement costs. It was apparent that the insurance costs also extended to the cost of insuring for business losses, which were outside the provisions of s 100 of the *RV Act*.

29. The transcript of the CTTT proceedings shows that the residents also argued that they should not be responsible for amounts representing unaccountable head office overhead expenses where the operator ran a number of like businesses in respect of which those overhead expenses whether for insurance expenses, or corporate recharge expenses, were

incurred in respect of the aggregate of those other businesses, and where the residents were not provided with the means by which to differentiate or to identify those items of expenditure or corporate recharge items that specifically related to their particular retirement village.

30. The CTTT transcript shows that the residents had argued, that as a result of those matters, they could not properly consider or approve expenses claimed in that way, as the expenses could not be transparently assessed as being capable of conforming with the agreed definition of properly chargeable outgoings.

31. The CTTT transcript also shows that the residents articulated a complaint that they should not be required to pay for such items on an arbitrary basis, which was the effect of the position adopted by the operator. The operator's position relied upon an averaging percentage or statistical approach to formulating the budget. That was advanced through the evidence of Mr Lam, Mr Burken and Ms Stephenson. That approach was described as "*fictitious* " or non-factual.

32. Significantly, in my view, the transcript does not reveal any request or formulation advanced on behalf of the operator, for the CTTT Senior Member to carry out a reasoned apportionment of such contentious expenses in order to meet the concerns of the residents. In this appeal, the burden is on the operator to demonstrate that the result of the CTTT proceedings was afflicted by an error concerning questions

with respect to matters of law. The absence from the transcript of a request made by the operator for the CTTT Senior Member to undertake a discretionary apportionment is a material consideration to the evaluation of the operator's attack on the reasons of the CTTT Senior Member concerning an alleged failure to exercise an available statutory discretion in favour of the operator.

33. The CTTT transcript shows that at the conclusion of submissions made by Mr Clarke on behalf of the residents, the following interchange took place between the operator's representative, Mr Burken, and Senior Member Jones:

"JONES: Thanks, Mr Clarke, okay anything else from you Mr Burken?

BURKEN: No I think, I don't want to contest a lot of those points which are accurate and inaccurate so I don't think its worthwhile going down - there's a number of inaccuracies and I won't attest to the applicants, I don't think this is the place."

34. Accordingly, if a means had existed by which the discretionary apportionments contended for in this appeal could have been identified in the CTTT, the evidentiary basis for the exercise of such a discretion was not provided to the CTTT Senior Member. The CTTT Senior Member invited further submissions, and in the course of his submissions, the representative of the operator did not make a request for the

exercise of the statutory discretion now claimed as an alleged failure. In my view, the absence of such a request of the CTTT to exercise the discretion now claimed, must be seen as being fatal to an appeal that seeks to rely on an alleged failure of the CTTT to exercise that discretion. The CTTT Senior Member had clearly taken the view that the two items in dispute were threshold matters to be considered on an all or nothing approach because he was not provided with a non-arbitrary evidentiary basis for making a discretionary apportionment as to what expenses were allowable.

Grounds of Appeal

35. The operator's summons which commenced the appeal, invoked 6 separate grounds of appeal. In my view, these can be conveniently condensed into the following formulations.

(a) Contended error in reaching a determination that excluded insurance and corporate recharge items from the budget, having regard to the contractual obligations that subsisted between the parties: *Grounds 1 and 2* ["the contractual grounds"] ;

(b) Contended error in failing to apply an apportionment of the insurance premium identified in the budget to reflect charges that were permissible pursuant to s 115(2) (d), (e), (g) or (h) of the *RT Act* , and a related contended failure to determine an approximate cost for that insurance: *Grounds 3 and 5* ["the insurance apportionment ground"] ;

(c) Contended error in failing to apply an apportionment of the corporate recharge item identified in the budget to reflect charges that were permissible pursuant to s 115(2)(d), (e), (g) or (h) of the *RT Act,* and a related contended failure to consider the provisions of regulations 17(1)(g) and 17(2) of the *RV Regulations* to determine and apportion the approximate costs of those items : *Grounds 4 and 5 and 6* ["the corporate recharge apportionment ground"] ;

36. A notice of contention was filed by the residents in the appeal. The notice of contention invoked s 199 of the *RV Act* , which provided that the operator was prohibited from contracting out of the provisions of the *RV Act* . The residents consequently argued for the unenforceability of the contractual obligations relied upon by the operator to justify the budgetary items in contention. The argument was to the effect that the insurance and head office expense items included in the budget, were not permitted by ss 100 and 112(3) of the *RV Act.*

Contentions of the parties

37. The primary submission made on behalf of the residents was that the CTTT decision was correct on its face, and involved no errors of the kind now claimed, on questions with respect to matters of law.

38. The submissions made on behalf of the operator were to the effect that the budget forecast items placed into contention by the residents were legitimate items of expenditure that it was

entitled to pass on to the residents. The operator further claimed that in its determination, the CTTT had failed to make relevant apportionments of such identified expenditure, including by analysing the evidence for that purpose.

39. The residents contended that the evidence placed before the CTTT by the operator could not have reasonably supported such an apportionment exercise. In contrast, the operator claimed that in these events, errors were made by the CTTT with respect to matters of law because of a contended failure by the CTTT to effect apportionments pursuant to statutory discretions that were available to the CTTT.

Argued errors concerning questions with respect to matters of law

40. In the appeal, the operator argued that jurisdiction for the appeal was established because, it was claimed, that the CTTT had made errors concerning questions with respect to matters of law in determining that the residents were not liable to pay the disputed amounts claimed by the operator.

41. In this regard, on behalf of the operator, it was argued that the CTTT had erred in that it had failed to exercise an available statutory discretion to interpret the evidence before it, in order to make an apportionment of the disputed budget items, and as a consequence, had incorrectly found in favour of the residents.

42. The outcome of the appeal is largely dependent upon the interpretation of the contractual documents entered into by the parties, as well as the relevant statutory and regulatory provisions, subject to the procedural matters that I have already identified as having arisen from the transcript.

Relief sought by appellant

43. The summons filed by the operator seeks orders to the following effect:

(a) The appeal should be allowed and the whole of the decision of the Tribunal should be set aside;

(b) The amounts of $23,100 for insurance, and $28,954 for corporate recharge expenditure, are to remain in the budget forecast for the retirement village;

(c) An order for costs.

44. There is an obvious tension evident between the grounds of appeal that alleged failure on the part of the CTTT to make an apportionment for the claimed budgetary items, and the relief claimed in the summons, which sought orders for the inclusion of the full amounts that had been claimed by the operator for insurance and corporate re-charge expenses.

Issues central to the outcome of the appeal

45. The central issue that was raised for determination in the appeal was whether, in reaching its decision, the CTTT failed to exercise statutory discretions that were available to it, in favour of the operator of the retirement village. The operator's contention is that the CTTT should have in some way apportioned the components of the identified categories of expenses as being payable to the operator by the residents.

46. The point that was at issue in the appeal seemed to be the contention of the operator to the effect that the exercise of such discretion was not only mandated in the circumstances, but that it ought to have been exercised in favour of the operator, notwithstanding the state of the evidence that the parties had placed before the CTTT.

Evidence before the CTTT and in the appeal

47. The parties had helpfully co-operated and had prepared an efficient common exhibit bundle which contained 61 separately tabbed categories of documents comprising some 333 pages: Exhibit "A". Those materials were identified as Exhibit "JS1", which was exhibited to an affidavit sworn on 8 March 2011 by Ms Jessica Carly Smith. Ms Smith was one of the solicitors acting for the operators of the retirement village.

48. Rather than here describe the large number of individual documents within those categories of papers, some of which proved to be of only background relevance, I will instead only

refer to the relevant parts of the documentation, where it becomes necessary to do so.

Residents submissions

49. The specific complaints of the residents were twofold. The first complaint was the legitimacy of the claimed obligation that they should meet the budget item of $23,100 in respect of insurance. Of this amount, the residents claimed not all of that sum represented a cost that could be fairly passed on to them: s 100 of the *RV Act* . The second complaint related to a claimed obligation that they should meet the forecast expenses in the sum of $28,495 which were described as corporate recharge items, representing categories of expenditure for administration costs, finance costs, human resources costs, property management costs, information technology costs and operations costs.

50. Dealing first with the insurance issue, the evidence disclosed that the claimed amount of $23,100 was a global quotation obtained and presented by an insurance broker and which related in part to the material cost of reinstatement of buildings and the like, to the value of $36,450,000 if certain defined events occurred to cause physical loss and damage. The evidence also disclosed that the policy quotation was to also cover potential consequential business losses and business interruption expenses for a period of 36 months if those defined events occurred.

51. The residents argued that the business loss component of insurable risk was not part of their contractual responsibility. The quotation identified these two areas of risk, but made no attempt at differentiating them in terms of apportionable premium costs. The residents submitted that the evidence which the operator had submitted to them, and later to the CTTT, was not capable of permitting a reasoned differentiation of those two components in terms of premium apportionment or allocation. The residents adopted the formulation that arose in argument, that these two metaphorical eggs could not be unscrambled as the quotation for insurance was a global one, which covered matters beyond damage to property and reinstatement thereof, and therefore, it should not be visited upon the residents in that undifferentiated form.

52. The residents also claimed that the relevant legitimate insurance costs that were contemplated as arising within the legislative scheme of the *RV Act* , were necessarily confined to insurance in respect of matters referred to in s 100(2) of the *RV Act* , whereas the expenses sought to be passed on to them by the operator went beyond those entitlement limits, and were not permitted by the statute in the context of consumer protection legislation..

53. The residents also claimed there was a lack of transparency in the proposed insurance charges, arguing that it could not be

properly or reasonably assessed or ascertained as to whether or not the proposed insurance costs covered legitimate items of risk, because the identified premium remained undifferentiated, and was therefore opaque to analysis.

54. With regard to the corporate recharge items in dispute, the complaint of the residents was that on the evidence, the items in question were not presented as being factually or temporally applicable to their particular retirement village, but rather, they were percentages of undifferentiated items that related to the overall business of the operator. The expenses were calculated as averages and percentages. The operator sought to impose them as a liability of the residents according to a formula, based on percentages, rather than being factually based expenses that related to the anticipated expenditure associated with the particular retirement village to which these proceedings relate.

Operator's submissions

55. The position taken by the operator in the CTTT was that it was entitled to levy the insurance costs and the recurrent charges under the statutory and regulatory scheme within which it operated.

56. The operator argued that as a matter of recognised business efficacy and efficiency, the governing legislation contemplated that an operator may operate more than one retirement village.

The operator also pointed to the mechanism within the legislative scheme for the preparation and approval of budgets for each retirement village separately. The operator submitted that regulation 17(1)(g) of the *RV Regulations* contemplated the apportionment of expenditure to a particular village as a proportion of a greater total and it was submitted that it had appropriately followed all proper steps contemplated by the legislation.

57. The operator also pointed to the fact that each of the residents had entered into an Agreement to Lease. Reliance was placed on the condition of the lease that provided for the residents to pay defined outgoings in the first schedule to the Memorandum of Lease. I have already cited the substantive terms of the definition of outgoings at paragraph [7] of these reasons.

58. The operator submitted that the expenses it had proposed to the residents in respect of insurance and corporate recharge items, which comprised administration, finance, human resources and information technology, were also properly identified as outgoings to be passed on to the residents pursuant to the agreement that existed between them.

Legislation and policy considerations

59. Variations in recurrent charges for retirement villages are defined, and require notice by the operator: s 107 of the *RV*

Act. Notified proposals for variations do not take effect unless the residents consent to them, or if the CTTT orders that they may have effect: s 107 of the *RV Act* . These provisions were obviously directed at consumer protection.

60. On any application to the CTTT for a determination in cases such as this, the CTTT is invested with the power to order that the proposed variation either take effect, or not take effect as the case requires: s 108(2) of the *RV Act*. In reaching any determination concerning whether variations should, or should not take effect on a consideration of s 108(2) of the *RV Act* , the CTTT is permitted, but not mandatorily required, to have regard to the factors outlined in s 108(4)(a)-(g) of the *RV Act* . Those provisions refer to market factors or conditions in the industry, levels of costs and services for providing the facilities, whether the residents consent to certain costs, the cost of general services, the frequency and amount of past variations, and "*any other relevant matter* ".

61. In a case where the residents have refused to consent to proposed items of budgetary expenditure, on the application of an operator or a resident, the CTTT is invested with wide powers: s 115(2)(a)-(i) of the *RV Act* . Again, those powers are discretionary in their application, and not mandatory. In particular, in the determination of a relevant dispute, the CTTT is given a discretion to make an order that the operator should remain liable for so much of the proposed expenditure as was

considered by the CTTT as being not reasonable or not necessary to pass on to the residents: s 115(4) of the *RV Act* . In making any determination under this section, the CTTT was given a wide discretion to have regard to " *any other relevant matter* ": s 115(6) of the *RV Act* .

62. I construe the references to " *any other relevant matter* " in ss 115 and 108 of the *RV Act* , to be read subject to the rules of procedural fairness, which, in this context, requires that appropriate notice be given to the affected party, and for that process to be applied, transparent evidence should be available in respect of any such matters to be considered in that regard. These conferred discretions are wide in their nature and effect. Accordingly, the exercise of such discretions must proceed according to recognised principles of fairness to the persons affected: *House v The King* [1936] HCA 40; (1936) 55 CLR 499.

63. The *RV Act* and the *RV Regulations* , being the legislative scheme under which this dispute arises, not only facilitate the provision of important social benefits and standards concerning the living arrangements for retired persons, but in recognition of the potential financial and other possible vulnerabilities of retired persons, it also contains significant elements of consumer protection: Hansard , *Retirement Villages Bill 1999,* Second Reading.

64. The social policy behind the scheme does not seek to impose an unfair burden on operators, as it recognises that the business of providing facilities for retired persons should be permitted to be profitable for the operators: Hansard , *Retirement Villages Bill 1999*, Second Reading.

65. Similarly, the policy behind the scheme for the operation of retirement villages does not seek to create an unfair advantage for the clients of operators. This is evident from the requirements that centre around the obligation of residents to pay for certain defined categories of expenditure that are incurred by operators, subject to compliance with identified administrative pathways.

66. In the context of the legislative scheme, the CTTT has been assigned the role of resolving disputes in a transparent and fair manner, or not in a manner that is arbitrary or unfair to a party.

Principles of interpretation

67. Insofar as it is necessary to construe any relevant provisions of the contract between the residents and the operator, the applicable principles of contractual interpretation are well known, and can be briefly stated.

68. In giving business efficacy to the terms of the agreement, the required approach is to consider what a reasonable person in the position of the other party would have understood the contract to mean in the context in which it was intended to

apply: *Toll (FGCT) Pty Ltd v Alphapharm Pty Ltd* [2004] HCA 52; 219 CLR 165, at p 179, [40]. In this case, this must mean balancing the relative interests and needs of the residents and the operator.

69. This requires that a literal, technical, artificial or overly syntactic or semantic based analysis that yields absurd results is to be avoided in favour of more purposive conclusions that reveals business common sense: *Antaios Compannia Naviera SA v Salen Rederierna AB* [1985] AC 191, per Diplock LJ at 201.

70. In construing relevant statutory provisions, the purposive interpretation is also the preferred or required approach in order to achieve the benefit intended by the legislation, recognising that in the context of this case, the *RV Act* and the *RV Regulations* contain significant consumer protection provisions. At the same time, the purposive approach to interpretation also requires recognition of the need for operators of retirement villages to be able to continue their operations profitably. However, in the context of a consumer protection statute, profitability is not the dominant consideration and fairness to consumers is at least a dominant balancing consideration to be weighed in the exercise.

Consideration

71. In the paragraphs that follow, I set out my consideration of the general, contractual, insurance and corporate recharge grounds in the appeal.

General consideration

72. In the context of this case, a purposive and business efficacy approach requires a balanced approach where acknowledgment must be given to the predominant features that contain compliance codes and limiting circumstances for the financial exposure of residents, purposively aimed at consumer protection. In my view, the fairest manner in which these objectives are met is for determinations and interpretations to proceed transparently on identified facts in evidence.

The contractual ground

73. In my view the contractual grounds of appeal can be disposed of simply. The definition of " *outgoings* " in the agreement between the parties requires that the changes sought to be made are " *properly and reasonably assessed charged or chargeable ... in respect of* the retirement village *or in the conduct management and maintenance of* " the retirement village. Where the contractual definition of outgoings makes reference to " *all* " expenses, that has to be read subject to the statutory provisions and the notion of reasonableness based on analysis.

74. By definition, these outgoings must be assessed by reference to the particular village in question, and not by reference to an artificial formula that has no particular application to the retirement village. The term " *reasonably* " must be given the contextual meaning that the charges should be capable of being reasoned to refer to the particular retirement village in a fair and sensible way, and factually particularised rather than being based on some other shared notion or estimate derived from considerations that apply to other entities, including the running costs of other retirement villages. The specific reference to Pelican Waters Village in the definition of " *outgoings* " requires that Pelican Waters Village be read as the definite article in such a consideration, and not some non-factual formulation when outgoings, costs and expenses are being sought from the residents.

75. In my view, that is the necessary common sense and business efficacy interpretation that must be applied in this dispute. The contrary interpretation, which seeks to impose charges not referrable to, or based on, the operations of Pelican Waters Village, is non-purposive, strained, not based on common sense and leads to the absurd and incorrect construction that would incorrectly equate generalities with the definite article : *Antaios v Compannia Naviera SA; Toll (FGT) Pty Ltd* .

The insurance apportionment ground

76. To succeed on the issue of apportionment of insurance costs, the operator's appeal must demonstrate a failure by the CTTT to exercise a relevant statutory discretion so as to amount to an error with respect to a matter of law: s 67(1) of the *CTTT Act* .

77. Any consideration of the relevant discretion conferred by the statute cannot be undertaken without reference to the facts that were in evidence before the CTTT.

78. The only relevant evidence that was placed before the CTTT on the insurance issue was the broker's quotation dated 21 September 2010. That document was addressed to Dollarvill Limited. The total cost of that quotation was in the sum of $48,851.98. The stated insurable interest was for material damage consisting of physical loss and damage to the property insured, together with consequential loss for business interruption. The policy provided for a limit of $50,000,000 in combined cover for these two nominated areas of potential loss. The quotation identified the respective cover for the values of the property insurance at $36,450,000, and gross profit insurance at $1,450,000.

79. Given the operator's complaint that the CTTT failed to apportion the insurance costs, it is relevant to look at the scope within the evidence for any such apportionment. In this regard, the two identified elements of insurance total $37,990,000. My purpose in identifying that total is to demonstrate that there appears to be no rational relationship between the insurance

liability limit of $50,000,000 and the combined cover values stated to be in the amount of $37,990,000.

80. Given that the amount for insurance that the operator sought the residents to pay was in the sum of $23,100, it is relevant to look at the quotation in order to determine whether the amount of $23,100 can be identified or explained by a reasoned reference to any of the abovementioned figures, either as to a finite part, or as a percentage of a greater amount: Exhibit "JS1", pp 179-183.

81. In this regard it is relevant to note that the insurance for which the quotation was obtained, was identified in the quotation as being for "Industrial Special Risks". The identity of the insured was stated as "Dollarvill Limited / Pelican Waters Village": Exhibit "JS1", p 181. The business description was "Principally Owners, Operators of Aged Care & Associated Facilities, Property Owners and other occupations incidental thereto": Exhibit "JS1",p 181.

82. Also of relevance is the nature of the insurance cover for consequential loss and business interruption. It was for gross profit, payroll, "gross rental or gross revenue if appropriate " and professional fees: Exhibit "JS1", p 181.

83. Also of relevance to the claim for discretionary apportionment of the insurance costs is the Australia-wide nature of part of the cover: Exhibit "JS1", p 183. The payroll component of the

cover was identified to be 8 weeks at 100 per cent, and 148 weeks at 30 per cent, with head office corporate salaries insured at 100 per cent for 156 weeks: Exhibit "JS1", p 183.

84. My purpose in reviewing the information set out in the preceding 8 paragraphs is to identify the dilemma that would have necessarily confronted the CTTT Senior Member in approaching any attempted form of rational analysis of this information for the purposes of trying to achieve a discretionary apportionment, as is now contended by the operator in this appeal. This analysis reveals that the following propositions would have been evident to the CTTT Senior Member:

Within the documentation in evidence in the CTTT, without explanatory evidence, the sum of $23,100 had no readily identifiable or rational relationship to the legitimate property insurance costs for the retirement village, as distinct from other, and unrelated expenses;

Any division of the sum of $23,100, or indeed the sum of $48,851.98, as insurance costs for proportionate relevance to the reinstatement costs for the retirement village, is completely opaque to an analysis that would enable a rational or reasoned discretionary apportionment. In my view, it is simply not possible to explain, with reasons, the manner in which a claimed discretion could be exercised according to the requirements of well-settled authority that precludes arbitrary results: *House v The King* .

85. In light of this analysis, without the required evidence, it was impossible for the CTTT to justify with reasons, any differentiation or discretionary apportionment within the identified insurance costs so as to confine that portion of the insurance costs that could reasonably be passed on to the residents as being proper or chargeable to residents in connection with the conduct, management and maintenance of the retirement village in question : *see contractual definition of outgoings* .

86. There is no doubt that the CTTT had jurisdiction to exercise a discretion on the question of insurance costs. However, in order for the operator to sustain its criticism of the CTTT concerning the contended failure to exercise that discretion in favour of the operator, a rational basis must be demonstrated to exist for the claim that the exercise of discretion ought to have been undertaken in favour of one party at the expense of another, on a non-arbitrary basis.

87. My review of the evidence before the CTTT on the insurance issue compels me to the conclusion that the state of the evidence simply did not permit any rational analysis of the insurance costs so as to enable a justifiable or reasoned apportionment of the insurance costs, including to confine such costs to only those costs permitted by statute as being legitimately relevant to insurance of the retirement village in question. Only the insurance costs permitted by statute could

be passed on to the residents: s 100 of the *RV Act*. That is not a provision which can be avoided by contract between the parties: s 199 of the *RV Act*.

88. In such circumstances, the CTTT was bound by the rules of procedural fairness and was precluded from arbitrarily exercising discretion in favour of the operator on any basis other than that which involved a rational analysis according to law. In my view the CTTT did not depart from that requirement. The question of whether the evidence permitted a rational analysis is a threshold question. It was either available, or it was not. If it was not available, the answer to the threshold question requires that there be no arbitrary exercise of discretion. The decision of the CTTT member must be seen in that light.

89. I therefore conclude that the CTTT Senior Member decided the matter of insurance correctly. In my view he correctly declined to undertake an arbitrary discretionary apportionment of the insurance charges: *CTTT decision, [56]*. In that regard, he correctly found the residents had no contractual obligation to pay the additional insurance charges for the risks in contention because there was simply no evidence that the risks insured were "*referrable to Pelican Waters Village*": *CTTT decision, [56]-[60]* . This was a simple exercise of assessing whether the evidence of the disputed charges was in conformity with the agreement. In my view, the CTTT

correctly decided the charges were not in conformity with the agreement with regard to the contractually defined meaning of "*outgoings*".

90. Accordingly, on that analysis, the CTTT Senior Member concluded that the undifferentiated claim by the operator for the disputed insurance costs should be excluded: *CTTT decision, [2]; [77]* . That conclusion is consistent with an analysis of the evidence in terms of onus of proof and the fundamental requirement of avoiding an arbitrary discretionary apportionment. I reject the submission that there had been a failure to consider a discretionary apportionment as an alternative to an all or nothing approach. My reason for so finding is that on the evidence, the CTTT Senior Member was left with the choice of an all or nothing threshold consideration, or making an arbitrary decision of apportionment. In my view, the state of the evidence mandated the former approach. The latter alternative was an unacceptable one and the CTTT Senior Member correctly recognised this to be the position.

91. In my view, the CTTT did not make any error concerning a question with respect to a matter of law on this issue. The insurance grounds should therefore be rejected.

The corporate recharge ground

92. The operator submitted that the contentious budget forecast items were legitimate items of expenditure that it was entitled to pass on the to residents. The alternative position adopted, was the claim that the CTTT Senior Member failed to exercise an available statutory discretion in favour of the operator, in order to apportion the corporate recharge expenses claim to identify an amount the operator could legitimately call upon the residents to pay, as properly chargeable items relating to the retirement village.

93. In my review of the transcript before the CTTT I have already identified the reasons why the apportionment claim is unavailable to the operator in this appeal to argue as a claimed question with respect to a matter of law: paragraphs [24] - [34] of these reasons.

94. In my view the failure of the operator to seek such an apportionment before the CTTT, and the failure to introduce evidence before the CTTT that would enable a reasoned analysis of what expenses were properly assessed or chargeable as referring to the conduct, management and maintenance of the actual retirement village in question, necessarily disposes of the corporate recharge ground of appeal.

95. The CTTT Senior Member dealt with the corporate recharge issue between paragraphs [61] to [71] of his reasons. He correctly identified the issue for determination as follows:

"61. The fundamental issue for determination is whether or not the amounts charged under the heading of corporate recharge are 'costs or fees <u>associated with providing services to residents</u> of <u>the</u> retirement village'. Unless the amounts included in the corporate recharge come within that exception provided for under Reg. 26(e) the operator is precluded from including the sum in the annual budget pursuant to s.112 and Regulation 26." [Emphasis added]

96. The CTTT Senior Member reviewed the operator's methodology for calculating an apportionment of Dollarvill Group expenditure on administration, finance, human resources, information technology and payroll. He also reviewed the evidence of Mr Burken, Mr Lam and Mr Stephenson on those matters.

97. The CTTT Senior Member correctly analysed Mr Lam's evidence by observing that as the operator's corporate financial controller, Mr Lam would be expected to have the knowledge or capacity to ascertain exactly what charges would be associated with the provision of the identified services to the retirement village to which this case related. He concluded, correctly, that information was not forthcoming: *CTTT decision, [65]* .

98. The CTTT Senior Member concluded on the evidence before him, that whilst it was self-evident that many of the functions for which the operator sought to charge the residents in fact related to direct or indirect services to residents, he also

concluded that he had insufficient information to determine that all the identified and claimed expenses incurred by Dollarvill concerning its overall operations, were appropriately apportioned to reflect a proper association to the residents of Pelican Waters Retirement Village: *CTTT decision, [66]-[71]* .

99. In view of the state of the evidence, for which the operator, as the applicant in the CTTT, bore the onus of proof, I consider that no proper basis has been made out for the assertion that the CTTT Senior Member relevantly failed to make a discretionary apportionment of the corporate recharge expenses, as is now contended on appeal. For the same reasons I have already identified at paragraph [90] of these reasons, I take the view that the all or nothing approach to this issue was the preferred approach rather than taking an arbitrary and inappropriate course.

100. Accordingly, in my view, no error has been demonstrated with regard to the claimed failure of the CTTT Senior Member to exercise his discretion to make an apportionment so as to raise an error concerning a question with respect to a matter of law.

101. The finding made by the CTTT Senior Member with regard to the corporate recharge issue was in the following terms:

"71. With the information available I am unable to say that the respondent was entitled to claim funding of the corporate recharge items from recurrent charges as claimed."

102. In my view, that finding, which required an all or nothing result, was compelling, and was the only proper finding that was available on the evidence. This was in circumstances where an arbitrary decision of apportionment would have been a legally unacceptable result. Accordingly, the corporate recharge ground of appeal should be rejected.

Disposition

103. I have determined that the operator's appeal should be dismissed on all of the grounds that were raised. In my view it should follow that the operator should pay the costs of the appeal incurred by the residents. In such circumstances, those costs should be paid on the ordinary basis unless, the residents can show an entitlement to an order in different terms.

Orders

2. I make the following orders:

   o (1) The appeal by Pelican Waters Village Pty Ltd is dismissed;

   o (2) The orders made on 9 December 2010 by the Consumer, Trader and Tenancy Tribunal in proceedings before it numbered RV 10/28914 and RV 10/31794 are confirmed;

- o (3) Pelican Waters Village Pty Ltd is to pay the costs of the Pelican Waters Village Residents Association on the ordinary basis unless otherwise ordered;

- o (4) The exhibits may be returned;

- o (5) Liberty to apply on 7 days notice if further orders are required.

....

Chapter 19

Conclusion

On Friday, 10th Jack distributed the following report to the letter box of each Pelican Waters resident.

To the Residents of Pelican Waters Village

Dear Fellow Residents,

As your elected representative in the District Court Appeal matter between Pelican Waters Village Pty Ltd and the Pelican Waters Village Residents Association, I report as follows:

The Hearing was held on the 14th and 15th March and concluded on the 8th April. The result was a resounding win for the Residents with Judge Lewis making the following Orders:

***1.** The appeal by Pelican Waters Village Pty Ltd is dismissed;*

***2.** The orders made on 9 December 2010 by the Consumer, Trader and Tenancy Tribunal in proceedings numbered RV 10/28914 and RV 10/31794 are confirmed;*

***3.** Pelican Waters Village Pty Ltd is to pay the costs of the Pelican Waters Village Residents Association on the ordinary basis unless otherwise ordered;*

The result of the findings of the District Court confirm that the line items of Insurance $23,100 and Corporate Recharge $28,594 (a total of $51,694) are to be removed from the 2010-11 budget.

It is my opinion this case will now set a precedent in law on at least the following points:

1. Residents only have to meet the cost of Insurance for the items related to in the Act.

2. In respect to the budget, Residents are entitled to receive sufficient detailed information so as to enable them to make an informed decision as to the acceptance or rejection of the budget. The information must show that the statement of proposed expenditure relates directly to services provided to the operation of this village.

At a recent meeting between your Residents Committee and Landbuild representatives the question was asked of Henry Wilson, "What will Landbuild do if the District Court Judgement is not favourable to the company?" Henry Wilson's reply was, "We would not Appeal the matter to a higher authority". I would like to think that we can take the word of a man of the calibre of Henry Wilson.

I acknowledge the assistance given to me in this matter by Shirley Dunlop, Bob McTavish and the Pelican Waters Village Residents Committee, together with several other Residents. Also, without the support received from you, my fellow Residents in resolving to see this matter through to the end and to not giving in to the threat of huge legal costs that may have been imposed upon us had our defence of this matter not been successful has been vital. The reputation of the Residents of Pelican Waters Village as being a group that will stand up for their rights and not give way to the intimidation tactics of a large company with unlimited resources is now legendary throughout the retirement village industry.

In the past two days I have received many phone calls and emails, all offering congratulations and expressing admiration for the Pelican Waters Village Residents' determination to see the matter through to the end.

Full credit and our thanks must be extended to Peter Hill of Hill & Co Lawyers, who so capably carried out our defence of the Appeal. Peter and his Staff gave our cause their fullest attention. Their expertise and knowledge of the Retirement Villages Act and Regulation left nothing to be desired, and their preparation of legal documents was first class. A job well done.

I must also acknowledge the support given to us by the Retirement Village Residents Association (RVRA). Without the participation of the RVRA our campaign in respect to having Landbuild offer to meet our legal costs would not have been successful.

The future success of the RVRA is dependent on a strong membership. The matter we have been involved in demonstrates that we, as Residents in a retirement village, must be represented by, and have access to, a strong and vibrant State

Association. The Association can only be strong and vibrant if we give it our fullest support.

Membership of the RVRA is only $15 per year for a single membership (less than 29cents per week) or $20 for a couple. Perpetual membership is available for $150 per single or $200 for a couple. Taking out Perpetual Membership means that you would remain a fully paid up member of the Association for as long as you reside in a retirement village.

It is exactly 12 months since this saga first began with a meeting between the Residents' Committee and Dollarvill representatives to discuss the 2010-11 budget. The matter has taken a large amount of Residents time and energy. A lot of time and energy is something that many of us do not have.

I am hopeful that we can put this episode behind us and look forward to working in harmony with our Management and Landbuild with the view to making Pelican Waters Village the village that a lot of people want to retire to.

Regards,
Jack Clarke,
10th April 2011

The above was followed by a bulletin sent out by the RVRA to its members:

The Final Chapter - Pelican Waters Village vs. Dollarvill / Landbuild

In December 2010, the CTTT made a decision in favour of the residents of Pelican Waters Village Laurieton, against Landbuild and the operator, Dollarvill Living.

Landbuild exercised its right of appeal and lodged an application, to be heard in Sydney on 8th February. Unfortunately, the residents were named as defendants and Landbuild said that they would claim legal costs against the residents.

In a great act of courage and determination, the residents of Pelican Waters voted to stay the course, and proceed with the case. **They would not be intimidated!**

The RVRA then waged a publicity campaign to politicians, on the internet and in the media.

On 2nd February, Landbuild rethought the situation. While the court case was still to go ahead, Landbuild offered to withdraw the demand for costs, and offered to pay the Residents' legal costs, up to $50,000. They also expressed their regret that they had not provided the degree of transparency in the budget, as required by legislation, and also about the way they had handled this matter.

On February 8th, Peter Hill, representing the Pelican Waters residents, with Jack Clarke as their spokesperson, and 37 members of the RVRA, attended the Directions Hearing in Sydney. The full case was set for March 14th 2011.

The hearing was held on 14th and 15th March. The residents had very welcome support from about 30 RVRA members. Because of some then unavailable evidence, the final hearing day was set for 8th April.

On Monday 4th April, Pelican Waters residents were advised that the operator was submitting an application to the Court for Discontinuance of the case. Although there were risks in continuing, the residents decided the principle was too important to comply. Peter Hill, Jack Clarke and the residents put together three excellent Affidavits, explaining that the principle was worth fighting for and that there were many villages depending on the outcome of this case to make their position clear.

Residents arrived at the court on 8th April, expecting to have a preliminary hearing on the Discontinuance. Once again the operator had changed its mind and had withdrawn the Application. In the Court, the Barrister for the operator said that the quality of the residents Affidavits made him realise his application would not be successful. The hearing continued.

At 3.45 pm Judge Lewis delivered a very short ruling –

The Judge:

DISMISSED the operator's Application to have the CTTT Decision of 9th December overturned;

UPHELD the CTTT Decision that the two line items in the 2010-11 budget, namely Insurance $23,100 and Corporate Recharge (Management Fees) $28,594 be removed. (This saved the Residents of Pelican Waters $51,694 this year).

The RVRA wish to congratulate the residents of Pelican Waters Village for their determination to see this important case through to its conclusion.

So, what are the implications for all retirement village residents?

In Peter Hill's view, these wider implications can be summarised as follows:

- *Operators must ensure that costs are broken down, identified and itemised for the residents to see the services they are receiving in their particular village.*
- *Attempts by operators to defray costs to residents by substantiating them on the basis of some artificial corporate wide formula, whether that be an averaging principle or otherwise, will not carry the day*
- *Reasons based on business convenience, or otherwise, of the operator in limiting the provision of information*

and inadequately identifying its relevance in the budgetary process, must give way to the principle of greater transparency for the residents.

- *Transparency as to what is being charged, how much, and how it relates to the provision of services in a particular village, needs to be justified;*
- *Operators are permitted to run multiple villages under the Act, but the apportionment of costs must be specific, actual and real to a particular village.*
- *Head office corporate or support charges that are claimed by an operator, must be based on the actual utilisation of services by residents in a particular village.*
- *The Act and Regulations have a strong bias toward consumer protection.*

Conclusion The success in the District Court is a significant win for residents across NSW.

Jan Pritchett,
RVRA Secretary

That afternoon at 4.00pm as was customary, Jack Clarke put a small cooler bag which contained a small bottle of scotch, a bottle of dry ginger ale, some ice and a glass over his shoulder and walked up to the meeting room where a group of men from Pelican Waters village would meet and over a drink or two would solve the problems of the world.

Jack walked into the room and most unusually all the usual participants were already there and as Jack walked in each man broke into spontaneous applause.   Then Jack noticed that on the table in front of where Jack normally sat there was a gift pack one litre bottle of 'Chivas Regal' Scotch whisky, there was also a printed certificate which expressed the appreciation of the group for Jack's efforts in representing the village residents.

When Jack sat down Michael Austin a man of few words offered Jack the thanks of not only the group assembled but each and every one of the Pelican Waters residents for the effort that Jack had put into the case. Michael then asked Jack, "Has the operator learnt anything from this matter, and have we learnt anything from the process?"

Jack thought for a moment then replied, "Well, I reckon that the operator and in particular Pierce Burken have learnt that just because the residents who live in their villages are old that does not necessarily mean that they are senile. If a residents committee asked a question about a village operational matter, such as 'what does the insurance policy cover?' then they have a right to an answer that gives them the information that they are seeking. The glib response of, 'That's a company operational matter and you don't need to know that' will not do".

"I believe that the decision made by the CTTT and the precedent set by the District Court in upholding that decision will benefit not only the residents in this village, but all retirement village residents throughout the State".

"We may have had a big win on this occasion; however, I don't believe that this gives us the right or the authority to be gung-ho in our negotiations regarding future budgets. I am of the opinion that if an independent mediator had been utilized immediately after the budget had been rejected then a compromise which was acceptable to both parties could have been reached".

"After going back over all of the material, including the transcript of the CTTT hearing I am convinced that Pierce Burken had an agenda, it may have been his or it may have been a direction from Dollarvill's senior management, but Pierce was out to show the residents that the operator was in charge and that we should just accept the fact".

"I am sure that if there had been a negotiated reduction in the insurance and corporate recharge line items of say, $5,000 at the initial Committee meeting when the budget was being discussed that would have been the end of it. Pierce Burken also had the opportunity to accept the committee's offer of a $15,000 reduction during the final negotiations at the Tribunal hearing. If some sort of conciliation above the $994 that was offered could have been arrived at then Dollarvill or Landbuild would have been about $250,000 better off. There was the insurance and corporate recharge that were removed from the 2010-2011 budget, our legal costs of $55,000, their legal costs would have been at least $100,000 and then there was the time and effort that their staff would have had to contribute to the matter".

"Anyway, it's been an interesting experience; however, one that I would not want to go through again". With that said Jack took the bottle of 'Chivas Regal' from its pack and taking the top off said, "I'm not going to take this home and drink it on my own, you fellows had better help me get rid of some of it now". And so they did.

At 5.35pm Secret Men's Business broke up and each participant headed towards their respective homes. The sun was just setting and a near full moon was rising as Jack Clarke walked, perhaps a little unsteadily home he notice in the sky above a pelican which was circling above Pelican Waters village. Jack stopped and watched the bird for a minute or so and thought to himself, "Yes, if there is reincarnation, I think I would like to come back as a pelican here at Pelican Lake and then I would be able to keep an eye on 'my village'.

The End

www.ingramcontent.com/pod-product-compliance
Lightning Source LLC
Chambersburg PA
CBHW051441170526
45166CB00001B/64